Path of the Heart

Path of the Heart

Beverly Lanzetta

PARAGON HOUSE
NEW YORK

Published by Paragon House
2 Hammarskjold Plaza
New York, N.Y. 10017

ISBN: 0-913757-64-0
Library of Congress Catalogue Card Number:

To My Parents

Contents

Foreword

Beverly Lanzetta has written a modern spiritual classic. *Path of the Heart* points to the simple core of an immensely mysterious reality. She points to the human heart, that mindful center and unifying bearer of insights, compassions and joys, common to the spiritual paths of all the great world religions.

The book is a modern classic because it reflects the global character of our contemporary religious situation. Ours is the first generation to inherit the communal heritage of the world's spiritual traditions. Each of us lives daily with the reality of the convergence of spiritual traditions in a pluralistic world. Will this convergence be one of conflict or peace? Will this be a time of great religious wars? Will warrior spiritualities dominate again; or can we find a new harmony, a new era of understanding on our road to that peace held within the Ultimate Mystery? Can we discover that in which peoples of good will place their faith, and thus their deeper trust? For our present challenge is to affirm both the Many and the One.

The book is a spiritual classic because Beverly has discovered through her experience a Divine Heart, in which her deeper self becomes a microcosm of the world's self. And thus she discovers not only a transcendent God, but a God of the soul, of nature, of interpersonal relationships, of the cosmos—an earthly or incarnate God if you will. This is a book that affirms rather than denies life, as the way to the Ultimately Divine. It is a book that calls its readers to grow in courage and expand in consciousness, and thus to be transformed in a simple happy wisdom. The author invites her readers to encounter this wisdom—Sophia, who is that lost feminine awareness of the inherent unity and wholeness of life. This is the enlightenment that has both a still point at its center, and a constantly expanding reality at its horizon. Love begetting loves. Mind begetting minds. Joy begetting joys.

As I read *Path of the Heart* I am reminded of the 12th Century and its love mystics. Bernard of Clairvaux, Richard of St. Victor, the Chartres School made the French Christian experience of that time such a universal one. At the same time we see Moslem sages such as the Spaniard Ibn Arabi and others overflowing with the gifts of an all transcending Love. Another Spanish mystic, Baya Ibn Paquda, a Sephardic Jew, spoke of "the duties of the heart, which embrace the realm of conscience, and this represents the science of inner life." In India during the same century the Alwai mystics of the south came to life with the love wisdom tradition that gave birth to the great Bhakti movement of Advaita love spirituality—now so much the dominant Indian way. Like the Maitreya Buddha this book sees the higher calling to be a rejection of Nirvana in order to return back into the world as a hopeful, compassionate servant for others. This is no escapist—flight from the world—spirituality. Quite the opposite it demands a practical conscience and an active service to alleviate the suffering of others. But it never forgets that peace begins with *me* and not just with *them*.

Path of the Heart is not a book about world spirituality but a book of world spirituality. It is a joyful lover's tale told primarily by the Beloved. Beverly's Beloved is the source of a universal way because Beverly's Beloved created the Universe itself out of a Love that knows no understanding, yet is all understanding. This is the Divine Reality that is the very hunger and longing for completeness that we feel and which only God fulfills. *Path of the Heart* is a call for each of us to live the destiny of this Love, all in All, love in Love, joy in Joy. It is a call to a beatitude of communion, of relationship, of sharing in the sacred community of the people of God. It is a call to be transformed—to be turned around, converted to a conscious path that asks us to depart the awareness that sees things only as separated, independent, adversarial and to add to this conscious path a straighter, broader path up the mountain—one that sees things as mutual, interdependent and complimentary—in Love.

Path of the Heart is also a book for those whose spirituality is secular. For the breakthroughs of new science have taken us into the relational consciousness of quantum physics, and the morphogenetic field theories of form biology pointing to the deep interconnectedness of our material universe. Scientific method is leading to communion and is more and more rooted in a respectful awe for the immensity and mystery of the cosmos that increasingly illumines modern scientists. Science is now far beyond the mechanistic reason of its outdated empiricism. The theme of reverence for life that has engaged so many humanists is receiving a new and deeper impetus as the vastness of human potentials are uncovered by new brain-mind research, biofeedback training etc. One also becomes aware of the incredible possibilities for reconciliation with the Marxist world, as we strive together to share our human stewardship of the earth, that sacred ground of our mutual hopes and strivings for the good life. This is a book that affirms the dignity of human life and offers a new basis for healing our wasteful secular-sacred divisiveness; in a new and deeper contemplative awareness that goes beyond God talk or anti-God talk, to a new and deeper contemplation of the human; to a more universal language for the ultimate mystery of this human earthly life; and to a new and freer surrender to the authentic sources of energy, creativity and care. The author shares with the human family an ardent desire for a universal wellspring of legitimate power and greatness, and admits to the kind of humility and discipline that its attainment demands.

For whether we see ourselves as belonging to either a sacred or secularist school, we share a common compassion for our brothers and sisters who are poor, hungry, homeless, imprisoned, lonely, beset by war and violence, or prejudiced against. "We are the world" say the words of the Africa relief song. We sing this inspiring song together because we feel compassion, we have a heart, and we follow its path that has its own bewildering conscience and understanding. "We are the world" for we are of the earth, of its consciousness and its stewards for good or evil. The earth is our common land and we humans its only people. In the words of the former Secretary General of the United Nations, Dag Hammarskjold, "God does not die when we cease to believe in a personal deity but we die when our lives cease to be illumined by a wonder beyond all reason."

Our present nuclear crisis clearly reflects the absence of that loving joy of which Beverly speaks. As a modern man threatened by man's modern destructiveness, I find myself cast back on the perennial message of the great myth of the Western world, Homer's *Odyssey*. This ancient text's concluding passages point directly to peace—our most urgent task. Beverly has recognized, with Goddess Athena of the epic, that "indeed they would have killed everyone, and prevented them from getting home again." This book is an echo of Athena's compassionate protest, "Men of Ithaca cease this dreadful war, and settle the matter without further bloodshed." But our author is first and foremost a spokesperson for a positive, concrete way to peace. If we heed her words our present crisis of human survival will have the happy ending of the Odyssey.

On this, pale fear seized everyone; they were so frightened that their arms dropped from their hands and fell upon the ground at the sound of the goddess' voice, and they fled back to the city for their lives. But Odysseus gave a great cry, and gathering himself together, swooped down like a soaring eagle. Then the son of Cronus sent a thunderbolt of fire that fell just in front of Athena, so she said to Odysseus, "Odysseus, noble son of Laertes, stop this battle, or Zeus will be angry with you."

Thus spoke Athena, and Odysseus obeyed her gladly. Then Athena, in the form and with the voice of Mentor, presently made a covenant of peace between the two parties.

Path of the Heart is a model, a way, a resource and a profile of Peace. Homer's eagle is our reminder. In the Christian tradition the mystic John the Evangelist has always been symbolized by an eagle. John's consciousness soared like an eagle, seeing the earth like a modern astronaut—as one. But John discovered this consciousness, by passing through the fiery thunderbolts of destructiveness, within the intimacies of his own heart. It was to John that Christ gave his final legacy, "Peace is my parting gift to you, my own peace, such as the world cannot give. Set your hearts at rest and banish your fears... Dwell in my love."

This is a book that is open to the Divine Mentor no matter what your spiritual tradition, be it secular or religious. It heeds the warning of a flaming holocaust and turns back to the earth—to the Divine Mother, and to her faithful, abundant and joyful path of the heart.

Richard J. Payne

Introduction

Spirituality is an infinite progression into the heart of joy. Our destiny is ecstasy. Unfortunately, one of the most basic misconceptions about the spiritual journey is that it is unattainable, and that it maintains a distinct identity separate from the one who seeks. Nothing could be farther from the truth. Rather, we are patterned of it. We excavate its unique character through the archaeology of our souls. In so doing, we draw deeper into the heart of God directly, joining life at a more profound level. Thus, the spiritual path is the medium through which we personally unravel the hidden workings of the universe. Although each path is individually unique, the pattern of spiritual life transcends the person and engages the seeker in the dynamics of a larger truth. The spiritual path is one that cannot be learned *about*. It can only be experienced. As such, life experience is the crucible in which we flame the pattern of divine nature.

Patterns

Three elements are consistent within the spiritual life. First, it is a life of which we are *composed*. The pattern we seek is the very "stuff" of our existence. We are made of it, as water is made of two hydrogens and one oxygen. The understanding of our destiny arises only as we understand the nature of what we are made. All human experience, then, becomes a progression into the heart of this truth. As spiritual seekers we are required to unravel any impediments which stand between our mortal selves and our beloved.

Secondly, the heart of spiritual life is joy. The pattern of existence is created through joyous rapture. As we are drawn deeper into divine nature, we imbibe life's happiness. Joy is the common denominator, the non-reducible element in the universe. Nothing of a lesser nature can comprehend the immense beauty and passion which activates creation.

These two aspects of the spiritual journey lead us to an important third element: It is impossible to not attain oneself, and hence spiritual joy. Certainly the ego may impede progress or deny it all together. The mind may resist, citing the impossibility of such a feat. Fear may intrude, as well as social customs and religious doctrine which may dictate restrictions on one's progress. Also, time cannot be a factor in spiritual growth, for it may take one individual eons to comprehend such lessons where another may learn in a short time. However, despite all resistances, schools of religion, philosophy, and science, the spiritual path will erupt within us. It must, of it we are composed. No sin is too great, no error too vast to prevent the expression of our highest destiny. This is the nature of joy. We are grounded in the basis of our divinity and we can attain nothing less than that, no matter how hard we try nor how long it takes. Ultimately, we will become One.

Universal Quality of the Spiritual Path

Spirituality is the shared language of the world. This is true insofar as it forms a common ground of knowledge which rests beneath the particularistic distinctions of culture, race, religion, or nation. Spirituality is a universal medium of expression and as such, it is a language we all know how to speak. Although we may have forgotten the most rudimentary exercises of our spiritual tongue, its melody remains forever within our memory, waiting to be awakened. We all know and resonate with this language for it is the birthplace of our souls. Thus, the spiritual journey is our gateway to universal experience and is distinct from other forms of pursuit in holding as its highest authority that which transcends all structure and image—the absolute. Spirituality exists in a dimension wholly different (not separate) from the physical and moral rules imposed by human beings on each other. For this reason, many socially imposed customs impede the perception of spiritual life because they are contrary to the egoless and harmonious state of divine love. Knowing this truth reveals the profound quality of universal life and frees the individual from both the limits and temptations of the physical world.

The Path

There is a process and a distinct path on this journey toward joy. Insofar as one is actually going deeper and deeper into the self, it is inaccurate to conceive of the journey as a linear progression. The path is cumulative. Patterns tend to repeat themselves in groups, each pattern building on the previous one. For example, let us consider five recognised stages in the mystical path: purgation, self-analysis, illumination, the dark night, and union. These five stages, rather than leading to one linear progression, occur in cumulative spirals. For example, one may work through level 1 of purgation, self...and come to level 1 of union. This insight then prepares the self to tackle the next level of purgation...etc. until the soul transcends the pattern itself arriving at the apex of ecstacy—where only joy and beauty exist.

The purpose of the cumulative spirals is to spiritualize the body. Since what we seek is within us, the main emphasis of all spiritual work is the refinement and strengthening of joy through a process which dissolves the impediments of the ego.

We are attempting, therefore, to illuminate our fears, our shortcomings, our hopes, aspirations, and limitations in the light of the absolute. In so doing we become wedded to a higher truth and join the pattern of spiritual evolution.

We begin with a self whose center is the ego and the physical universe. This self believes in its own mortality and fears confrontation with death. This self holds onto the social, religious, cultural, or particular historic scene of his or her life, and measures life in relation to these beliefs. A person at this stage would find his or her identity deeply intertwined with the survival of his/her religion, race, nation, personal views, etc. In the progression from physical to spiritual person, there are innumerable subtle stages which take the individual from an ego-centered reality to a God-centered one, and then beyond to union with the absolute, where no image takes hold.

The path has its markers as one progresses through stages of spiritual development. The method, however, is not all important. What is important is the sincerity of the quest, and the longing to know God. Once the individual is strong about these convictions, one has taken a first step in standing outside the ego. Now, there is room for the universe to hold hands with the seeker. Each true longing for truth resonates a prayer into the depths of one's consciousness, sparking the memory of our spiritual language. Buried deep within the recesses of the heart are the sacred emotions which have lain dormant and which now propel the seeker toward greater understanding. What one is compelled to do, is to relinguish all negativity, for negativity suppresses the joy which wells within the spiritual heart.

The most miraculous aspect of the path, however, is that it

is impossible not to achieve one's desire. As ye ask, so shall ye receive. Intense, pure, longing will bring one to God. Whether it takes years or lifetimes, each individual is drawn to the sacred self, from whence one has never known separation. Knowing this fact dismantles the despair, the doubt, and the powerlessness we humans carry. Negative emotions are based on a relativistic notion of reality, borne from an ego-centered view of the universe. Despair and doubt arise from a belief that the individual has control over the ultimate nature of things. That is, a person believes whether he or she doubts the existence of spirit, or despairs of his/her ability to get there, has a bearing on the existence of such a state. Or, that despair is real, and is an ultimate statement of one's potential. However, these are merely misconceptions of the physical world.

The Heart

We are now faced with a pivotal and most important question: Through what medium or mechanism does one pursue the path? The mind, being trained, is a tool for analysis and for seeking the limits of things. It deals with the concrete, the beginnings and ends, and with the packaging of reality. The mind exists in the realm of images, beliefs, and structures. It is not equipped to assimilate the infinite in total. By nature, the mind must break down the component elements of its subject and reshape these elements into a decipherable whole. Despite the level of analysis, whether the most physical or the most etheric, the mind will impose a structure and a form. Hence, what the mind perceives will be limited in scope by its own nature.

Yet, it is possible to partake of infinity. This is the path of the mystics, or those who through chance or through grace have touched the absolute. here, one unites with the wholeness of the infinite, if not the totality.

This medium without limit, assumption, or thought is the heart. It is through the spiritual heart that one comes to know the way of love and the path which leads to freedom. It is the heart which must be purged of pain and which must be strengthened to withstand the inevitable struggle with human sorrow. It is the heart which must be cleansed of emotional impurities so that love flows fully and without condition.

It is not sufficient to know with the mind alone. One must rummage through the pathways of the heart: its hopes, fears, limitations, and sorrows to know oneself, and thus, God. The universe exists within us, and the mechanism for removing human negativity is the heart. The heart speaks no judgement. Neither does it react nor specify limits. The nature of the heart is to be open, receptive, and unconditional. The heart is our divine medium and our window to the absolute. We need not seek the spiritual path with the mind, for the pattern of our divinity shall impose itself upon us. It beckons us, tapping on the closed corridors of our hearts. It is through the heart that we come upon divine passion, and the sparks of creation itself. Through the mind we know the law, but it is through the heart that we embody it. The intensity and profound objectivity of the heart is staggering. Because it stands outside of image, it is the most objective reality we know. And it is a truly uncharted territory of human potential.

This book, then, attempts to share the path as viewed from the heart. How does one proceed to the absolute using the heart, rather than the mind, as a guide? As one proceeds through the various stages of ascent, how does the heart respond, what are the markers and the sensations? It is a book which appeals to the heart directly, speaking in our common spiritual tongue. Hopefully, its message reaches across the barriers imposed by our mental limitation, touching our shared universality. It was written from a deep feeling of sharing, of joining our hearts in the pattern of joy and with a gratefulness to be able to do so.

The Methodology of the Heart

Those who seek true knowledge and the essence of universal truth will come upon that realm of the Heart, wherein begins enlightened quest. This Heart, oh wondrous beauty, reflects the magnitude of Divine Presence upon the residual fringes of human thought, cutting through the mind's tenacious hold and jolting the seeker into another realm. This realm is not of the world and finds small reflection on the physical plane. Yet so integral to human life is this miraculous

Reality that it resonates within the recesses of spiritual history, stirring the heart's memory of Something Wondrous and forgotten.

Without the Way of the Heart, existence could not come into being as all creation is sustained by the mysterious heartbeat of Life, pumping Love into form. The Heart is the prime mover and healer of human sorrows as it replenishes the spiritual bloodstream with Divine strength.

This Heart knows not of lust, greed, jealousy, or other human emotions. This is not the heart of human invention which resides within the paradoxes of cause and effect. This is the Heart of infinity's longing, this is Divine Love. Nestled silently within mortal breast the ever-present Reality awaits man's necessity for another Way and for the surrender that compels the opening of Love's door.

Simultaneously beating with human breath, the mystical Heart infuses the finite self with Divine attributes. Despite fear, pain, ignorance, or other frailties, this Great Heart remains bonded to physical form and nourishes the body throughout life's journey. Here, among the sorrows and erroneous paths, and here, amidst the desecration and the travail awaits the answer to human prayers, the infinite Love that heals all wounds and teaches one compassion and humility.

All humanity is sustained by the mystical Heart. All people share the inheritance of divine Love, which transcends the specificity of individual belief. Some hearts are wounded, some are fractured and spent; some suffer the illusion of separation and aloneness; others learn to constrict the passageway to Infinity—yet all instinctively know its Call and its Message. None escapes the Heart's divine claim.

Although the finite dimension is compelling and mesmerizes the soul into amnesic sleep, the Heart exerts a powerful force upon human consciousness. Never at rest, the self seeks the Presence behind the shadow it perceives, the dimly veiled remembrance of Something More. One knows there is more, one hears the faint whisper of Infinity's sigh, and one begins to yearn for communion with this intuitively known, yet unseen, Heart.

One now is ready to embark upon the journey of the Heart, removing the barricades which separate the mortal love from its Divine parent. One now is ready to battle the self-inflicted obstructions which tempt the mind and divert the heart's quest from Itself.

The Heart has its own Way. The mystical Heart belongs to God alone and does not adhere to any creed, religion, or sect. It transcends reason and stands untouched by mortal mind. The nature of this most holy Reality cannot be comprehended by the intellect nor contained within the limited system of human emotions. This Love touches all and knows the same Truth, being part of the fabric of Infinity's mysterious Light.

Because Love is pure and knows of no other, it infuses life with the capacity to rise above the finite plane of existence. The divine Love allows one the sight necessary to slice illusion from the heart and to reveal the beginnings of another Way. This Love is so purified, so much of itself, that it is the strongest weapon and the greatest force, stronger still than any physical prowess. It is the Light that pervades consciousness and germinates new life.

Within the infinite realms of the divine Heart exists the pattern of existence and the Way of Truth. Here in the longing for

Infinity and the devotional plea for God rests another way, a way much more rigorous and exacting than any on the mortal plane. This is the methodology of the Heart.

This method of the Heart underlies all action and forms the fundamental pattern of creation. In contrast to the scientific assumption of a separate observer, the methodology of the Heart arises out of union with All that Is and posits another kind of perception. Rather than approaching reality from the separatist, observational perspective of empirical science, the Heart demands union as a prerequisite and method for approaching the Unknown.

Both the method of science and of the Heart are a way of approaching the unknown, but more than a way, they postulate a set of conditions concerning the nature of reality itself. Although each discipline operates in seemingly distinct realms perceived to be vastly different by the mind, each is, in fact, utilizing the same method in unlocking the patterns of Reality.

Science explains how physical matter operates, just as mystics and prophets explain how spiritual reality works. Both explanations are scientific and use the same methods and the same kinds of analysis because both are describing different dimensions of the same Reality. The heart, however, does not assume an inherent separation exists between the physical and mystical domains. Mysticism, therefore, describes a more inclusive level of knowledge because it incorporates not only the method of the universe, but the passion and law as well.

The way of the Heart is a key to unlocking the workings of the universe and the solution to the ancient problems which plague humanity. The method of the mystic and the purging of the self in the fires of Divine Light illuminate the path which is the only way to truth. This is truly a method, a method as rigorous and as reproducible as any scientific one. This is a method that involves the core of humanity, it cannot be undertaken in the dispassionate quest of the empirical escape. This method demands the very blood of one's existence and the relinquishing of the protection objectivism finds in the sterile walls of empiricism.

Physical matter provides an observational system that does not require the abandonment of one's assumptions about existence. Until the recent discoveries in subatomic physics, the scientific method did not necessitate any fundamental shift in human perception. The observations of science allowed man to posit himself as separate from the workings of nature. And superior to it.

The mystical method knows better. It sees a reality that is uniformly operating and accurately balanced within all matter, from the most etheric to the most physical. The mystic knows that the only way to the core of Truth is through the surrender of the self to the method of the Heart. For only in surrender can one withstand the inevitable shock and enlightenment that will come upon the confrontation with the Unknown.

The universal message that has filtered through Time, from all the major religions and all the great prophets and saints, is the same. That is, all perceive a similar State and a State which cannot be arrived at through the mind alone. The mind is an insufficient medium for the discernment of Truth because the universe is composed not only of structures and functions but of divine emotion and passion as well.

It is the way of the mystic that unveils the road that must

be travailed to arrive at the solutions that face mankind. The mystical path is not confined solely to saints and visionaries, but rather serves as a pattern for all humanity. This path, which brings one face to face with divine Wisdom, is the same path which can illuminate the paradoxes of life and which can be used as a guide for the future evolution of mankind.

The mystical patterning begins with a longing for an answer, which often is overlooked in the complex mazes of today's world. This road insists on dedication and spiritual strength and forces one through the tunnels of illusion, despair, and ego. This overwhelming desire to Know, compels the seeker to confront those facets of human existence which impede the perception of God. Contrary to most belief, the mystical path is a path of scientific rigor and verifiable content. The mystic and the prophet are articulating an objective reality. In fact, they are describing the Only objective reality, a reality totally unbiased and factual, because it comes from no-one.

The path is objective, and infinitely fair. The tests one must endure are ones which will purify the mind and the heart and prepare one to receive this immense Truth. The Truth exists and so does the way to get there, but one must be willing to abandon the mind and all other securities of the physical dimension if one wishes to arrive at the juncture of the Heart.

The mystic, prophet, and healer share a similar journey, a journey which is directed by the heart alone and by the perception of another kind of reality. The willingness to accept the existence of this reality and to abandon oneself completely to a sphere so fundamentally different than the one defined as real, requires a commitment of courage and a true love. Throughout history one finds a similarity of experience in all the writings of the numerous ones who have walked a spiritual path. These shared experiences form a core pattern of behavior, which illuminates the learnings required to embark upon the methodology of the Heart.

The Way of the Heart is premised on the assumption that there is something to Know. That is, that something Universal exists which transcends history and in which one can find answers to the multitude of questions locked within human existence itself. This methodology does not say, however, what will be known, whether what is known has a purpose or meaning, whether the nature of the known is good or bad, finite or infinite. The Way of the Heart does not impose judgments nor predetermined conclusions. It simply seeks to Know, with all its being, with all its love.

Paradoxically, what the heart seeks is not separate from itself, and as such, the further unveiling of Truth compels the individual seeker into greater union with that which is being sought. The search for the Unknown entails the transformation of the one who asks, revealing answers and realities which could not be perceived by the unmetamorphosized individual alone.

In this state of surrendered quest, one comes upon the paradox of purpose in no-purpose and meaning in meaninglessness. One comes upon the essential quality each individual exerts upon the journey and the journey imposes in return. One comes to Know that only in the union can purpose and meaning be *experienced*, not thought and not postulated. *Experienced*. Here in the condition of oneness, there is neither thought not separate thinker, there is only the action of the condition itself. Here in union is true neutrality, pure science, and the unconditional willingness to neither impose historical limitations on experience nor to limit the expression of such in one's life.

The Heart has its own methods and its own tests. It is this methodology of the Heart, the precursor for all transcendent experience, that is explored in the following chapters and wherein one may find another path in the mysterious Unknown.

The Yearning

It is passion that instills the holiness and sparks the sacred power from Mystical Heart. This passion is the first condition for spiritual quest without which one would not have the fortitude to pursue God directly. For it is spiritual stamina and great strength that are essential for divine indwelling. This fortitude is one's Divine inheritance, yet like all attributes it must be developed, channeled, and refined to fit one's particular need. Spiritual strength knows not of mortal rules, nor seeks its answers upon earthly grounds. Spiritual strength resides within each creation, being the living flame of its existence. Yet, the flame may be subdued, damaged, hidden, or camouflaged beneath the fears, the sins, and the guilts. The flame can never die, nor be destroyed, for always it remains one and united with the Ultimate Source of existence.

Mystical insight involves the reaching within one's silent depths, calling forth the flame, the passion of creation's yearning for Itself. In this way, one beckons the strength within, fanning the flame of Divine passion, which is the first sustenance and birth of All That Is. Without this inner passion, this need, this longing for the Unknowable, this first and only search, one is not Real. To know Reality, one must come face to face with the passionate Need for Oneself. To attempt anything else, to study, to question, without this first essential condition being met, is to wander aimlessly with that which can stimulate only the mind. The mind, however, cannot lead one to God. Neither can the psyche. It is only within the Heart, wherein the infinite Passion emerges, can one find the path and the sustenance sufficient to guide one upon the treacherous waters and barren, solitary deserts of human ascent to the Unknown.

The yearning, then, becomes the first prayer: Please help me, Please show me the way, Please open my heart to Thy way, Please teach me Infinite Love. Longing is part of creation's sacred mystery. Without longing, without the fragrance of Divine Love, nothing Is. All Life moves within this simple state. Only humans set about the denial of emotion. Only humans enclose the holy perfume, afraid of its magnificence, afraid to be intoxicated, afraid that it may lead them outside themselves. Search without abandonment is not surrender. If one is not abandoned, there is no reason to seek, for as one seeks, so shall one find. Stagnated passion discovers small and petty gods.

Within all human situations, this flame of passion exists. It must exist, for without its burning Light, there is no creation. Therefore, as one breathes and moves, so does God within. To find this Truth, to gaze upon the infinite realms of mystery, and to know the sacred, one must throw the self upon the rich meadows of Infinity's longing for Itself. Only in this way, will one begin the development of true strength.

Longing is the heart's embrace, calling forth That of which there is no other. Longing is creative freedom, the willingness to relinquish all self-definitions for one's Love. This essential call, this necessary beckoning, is both instilled from God and nourished by human intent. One must actively seek longing's melody, as one would seek and master music, but simultaneously surrender the self to the movement of longing's ways.

Abandonment to Yearning diminishes the fear men harbor, that terrible sense of unworthiness. For in yearning, there is neither actor nor action, but only the endless tide of life's craving for itself. Here, one enters a new reality, another kind of existence, and one not premised on the separate, isolated self. Life's longing is both the gateway and the road to joy, for now one begins to partake of life, to roll with It, to engage in the ultimate and only action. One begins to glimpse the fringes of joy's immensity, and one knows that life is not alone.

As one embarks on yearning's call, one confronts the resistances and the fears that ward off man's first fragile attempts at self-knowledge. Demons are released, man's historical impotence, his accumulated despair, demons of unknown magnitude and ample certainty. These demons of mind's growing infiltrate the simple passion, the small and still voice within, ridiculing human unfolding as if one's desire could be controlled by mental feats. Yet humans, being both flexible and infinitely curious, conjure and construct the impossible. And so, negation stands.

One learns to hide, to sense embarrassment and shame, to cover the sacred longing, to diminish the timeless aloneness and the ancient sorrowful separation from nature's self. One learns there is not virtue in truth, no support for tender longings from the heart, nor physical sustenance in revealing the deepest grace. One learns to accept the small, mortal love, that parody of life's infinite possibility, for the greater need. One learns to substitute the finite for the infinite and the temporal for the divine. One learns to lose Self.

These resistances and trained responses weave the external fabric of daily life. They drown out the low and insistent intonation, the call for God, they drown out the soul's passion for Itself, and the heart's yearning for Home. Yet they cannot destroy that which one Is. They cannot annihilate the essential Beingness, the Life of all life. They cannot contain the hope, nor the faith, that humanity is already There.

It is the extent of one's willingness to embrace the passion which provides the necessary force, agility, and strength to cut through the many-layered illusion of human self-deception. For one must be willing to do battle to attain the Love. One must be willing to slay the small self for the possibility of greater self—God's longing for creation, and creation's longing for God—for herein lies the mystery of devotion, that pro-

found selflessness which forms the building reality of the
Nameless Infinite.

> Pray upon the yearning,
> Call forth the illusions
>   Of the mind.

> Step upon illusion's head,
>   crushing doubt and cynicism
> From the heart.

> Devote the self to the
>   passionate flame
> Which calls upon you.

> Then shall you be prepared,
>   step by step,
> For the greater unfoldment of
>   Divine Mystery,
> As you are strengthened and
>   fortified by each successive
> Battle and emerge victorious
>   over your Heart.

Strengths & Fortitude

Once firmly upon the road of passion, one comes to develop the strengths necessary to endure the steep ascent in God's Way. Spiritual strength is carved from within the passion, shaping and molding the emergent heart and preparing it for the fortitude that is essential for self-knowledge. It is the yearning that is a strength, a powerful ally in the continued quest for the Unknown. The yearning tugs on the heart, revealing deeper and deeper layers of life's infinity and as such prepares the self for the trials to come.

It appears paradoxical that the vulnerable and tender heart, pushed deeper and deeper into its own infinite longing, should serve as the most powerful and fundamental grounding for one's lessons in strength. Yet, it is the heart and its capacity for devotion, compassion, and giving that is the seat of divine strength, and without which there would not be the fortitude to seek the Truth.

Longing is a catalyst for courage, pushing open the doors of fear, timidity, and restraint. Longing dredges up the demons, not stopping to acknowledge them, and casts them into oblivion on its march back to Self. The longing makes one delirious with love, willing to attempt any task, and confident that one will survive the inevitable battle to ensue. Longing is one's strength for it draws one continually into the flame of life's unfolding, replenishing the depleted stock of bravery, and nourishing the fragile spark encased within human breast.

The trials themselves—the battles with the demons, the fear of annihilation, the anguish over possible misdeeds, the certainty of one's failure—are the tools and the methods for development of spiritual strength. They are the masterful benevolence which Knows the soul's secret quest and sets about developing a strong and resiliant spiritual personality. It is at this stage that the soul goes into training.

Each battle serves to illuminate and destroy the illusory film human emotions exert on Truth, clouding the perception and weighting the heart in a mire of sympathy and despair. The battles are real and so is the Joy. Each test only further pushes the heart into greater and greater turmoil for it MUST confront the disjuncture that exists between divine Reality and mortal construction. This tension between Infinity and finitude is the battleground for spiritual growth and upon which Yearning, in moments of blindness, will guide.

This vast disjuncture between Reality and mortal play is anguishing, wrenching apart the very foundation of one's thought and one's mind. Here the conditions of life appear surreal, there is neither bottom nor top, one's constructions are tossed gloating about, randomly and without seeming purpose. Here one experiences that the mind is not sufficient to center reality, that anything, ANYTHING—that is anchored in the mind alone or in the restricted dimension of a rigid heart is not Real and therefore destructible.

It is the survival of human ego that one battles, this facade of knowing and strength. It is the face-to-face confrontation with human illusion that is stunning, numbing the senses, and forcing the mind into smaller and smaller boxes until the mind, weary of its own mazes collapses, allowing in the passion again. Yet, the battles have only begun and each successive war will reveal the power of Divine Will and the weakness of human invention.

One cannot lose in this. For what is being destroyed, the unreal, the mortal construct, the social personality, is being replaced by the REAL, the divine essence, and the spiritual Heart. Yet, one grieves immensely. The poor delicate human heart convulses as it witnesses the enormity of the lie, the fact of human isolation side by side with the illusion sharing and love. The generations of struggle, the history of pain, the human toil, so noble yet so frail, the meaningless battles over religion, and the struggle for social supremacy weigh upon one's heart, fracturing the emotional balance, leaving one spent.

More painful still and closer to the heart, is one's own lies, one's own fears and fits of unworthiness, one's aloneness and bouts with meaninglessness. One has many battles left. Each lie of the self, each admission of doubt, of ultimate nothingness, only burdens the journey further, and without the Yearning, one would not have the fortitude to witness human deceit and to emerge whole in divine embrace.

As each trial is passed, and the fractured patterns of human invention are tossed upon the foam of the Holy Breath, one begins the development of true Strength. This is the Strength that ennobles the human spirit and elevates the self beyond the relative dimension. This Strength is the fabric and the pattern of Reality, without which one cannot perceive God.

The Strength never allows one to succumb to the illusion, it forces one to claim life's joyful inheritance. It demands perfection of vision, where one no longer can indulge the senses in the balm of forgetfulness. The Strength purges the heart, diving deeper and deeper into the abandoned crevices and the hidden valleys of Love's call, Passion's beckoning. The Strength reveals the Heart's power, which IS Strength, entwined mystery of creation.

As each battle is fought, Infinity observes. Is one weary? Does one succumb? Does one regress upon illusion's path? Or does one pull oneself up, yearning for more? Ready for the next trial, desiring to drink of eternal knowledge, and quench one's thirst? All this and more is observed. Only when the Yearning is intense, when it consumes all other possible endeavors, when the human heart and the divine heart touch, is one sufficiently fortified to perceive the hem of the Heart's mysterious garment. Now begin lessons in true Strength.

Strength is not aggression or willful attempt, neither is it restraint of emotion nor powerful display. Strength is a quality of Reality and as such embodies endless lessons rooted in the heart. From the heart great spiritual lessons emerge, developing the mystical strength that cannot be damaged or demeaned by offense. This is the strength that brings one upon the ladder of enlightenment, or that place where one is literally "illumined" by Wisdom which finally wrestle's mortal heart from illusion's grasp.

Mystical strength is premised on divine Love, wherein all great truths emerge. These are lessons of another kind, lessons of strength, where one learns to stand amidst doubt, deception, and ridicule, unmoving, without turning to flee, without shielding the self, and accept into the heart the wounds of unknowing. Here, in this state, the negation becomes a tool for one's further advancement, for each blow of illusion only serves to shatter one's own despairs.

Miraculously, as one shoulders greater and greater blows, yet does not succumb nor lose yearning's intent, the mortal heart melts away, revealing the beginnings of Love's journey. It is now neither possible nor desirable to turn away as Love begins to infuse the mystic bloodstream, rejuvenating the weary self. Love wishes to know, it seeks the Truth, and beckons injustice to its door. Love demands total attention and ultimate union with all that is pained, because only in union can the sorrow be lifted from human hearts.

Here, in this state, resides great mystical strength. As Love unfolds within mortal breast, one is blessed with a searing compassion which sees the suffering, the grief, and the injustice of the human condition. But more than seeing, the compassion acts, for total observation creates union from which first Action arises. The compassion is an active strength, it does not rest dormant within one's heart. It is a vital force which mends all pain, releasing joy into spiritual space.

Numerous trials will one endure in this condition, for the self still resides between two worlds: the finite and the infinite. Each surrender on Love's path, further purifies the heart revealing the vulnerable and virgin seed, man's divine inheritance. Yet, the more tender and of light one becomes, the more difficult is one's mortal regression and the more arduous and steep becomes the divine ascent.

Surrender now is essential. The more infused with Love's strength one becomes, the more one is equipped to surrender. Surrender is a special kind of power, a power that comes from being united with the Source of life, which replaces the ego's constructs with formless mind. The state of surrender is an immeasurable strength as one becomes flexible, able to tumble with illusion, even laugh at its foolishness and conceit.

Battles are still raging and the war is not yet won, but one's perception of the battles, and therefore the battles themselves, take on a new dimension. One begins to separate the Self from the illusion. The illusion still exists and still exerts profound hold upon one's heart, but the moments of awareness increase, and the certainty of being grounded in the joy takes on a reality of its own.

The many wounds, the humiliation of one's errors, the magnitude of human sorrow, the awesome splendor of creation, and all the other many trials and lessons function to increase the heart's capacity for joy. The pain, then, serves to shatter the mind's reality and all the multitudinous creations designed by limited mortal perception. As the finite and unstable is fractured, rigidity is replaced by flexibility and selfish love by surrender. And these are very great strengths.

To hold the joy within one's heart and to sustain the infinite upon mortal journey requires tremendous spiritual strength. The strength that understands yielding and surrender as tools for high insight and compassionate living, the strength that shoulders pain amidst the joy, and the strength that yearns for Love's healing touch are critical feats which must be mastered upon the road to the sacred.

The Path

There is a path and a journey, yet each is uniquely of one's own invention, being as varied in experience as there are those walking along its way. The similarity of paths rests not in the form nor in the function, but in the lessons that are learned as one embarks upon the mysterious quest. Despite the many possible roads to travel, the paths all lead to the same ascent: one which will strip illusion from the mind through the releasing of doubt, judgment, cynicism, and despair. Here on the road to the Unknown the individual ego will be wrenched from the mind, replacing the small self with union in divine purpose. And here, on the lonely plains of uncertainty and barren crevices of human conceit, will the heart be pierced with infinite mercy, compassion, and love; and the soul infused with the splendor of divine wisdom.

The power of the journey and the intensity of one's yearning propel one into an environment from which there is no longer escape. One is imprisoned by the soul's intense longing for freedom, a freedom which demands the path and the lessons. It is this thirst for freedom that fortifies the weary traveler and activates the curiosity and desire for the Unknown. Once one wishes for freedom above all else, there is no danger of falling off the steep ascent nor of losing one's way.

Still, the path has its markers and its tests. Without the shedding of the ego and the illusions which cloud the mind, one is not firmly planted on the road. Often one may not be aware that a mystical ascent awaits silently in the shadows of one's despair and lost hopes. The seeker may not know of what he seeks or if anything is sought at all. Yet the path stands and the freedom beckons all, however blindly, to its doors.

What is the path, then? Is it truly a road upon which one steps, moving ever closer to God? Is it a direction, a way one moves from one place to the next? Is it a method or a journey? Are there one or many? What is it?

Confusion reigns at this juncture, for one still imagines that the path to God should answer the call of the mind. The questions themselves make no sense on the Way, nor do they alleviate the suffering and the anxiety, but still the mind must ponder and sort for it is not yet weary of itself.

The mind does not rest, seeking to understand, understand. It never questions the source of its own understanding nor grows disenchanted with the answers it serves. The mind is fascinated with its own ability to postulate such profound questions. It is not the answers that are important to the mind, for no answers truly are sought. It is the capacity to utilize the mind that captures one's attention. In fact, many are wandering still along this path of the mind's invention.

This web of the mind paralyzes the fragile quest, diverting its attention into corridors of deception. Those who are dazzled by the mind's brilliant creations remain trapped within the structure of thought, impervious to infinity's call. They no longer yearn for freedom because they mistake the maze of mental edifice for the endless wonder of creation. These individuals are no longer on a path, they have arrived. At the abode of the mind.

Others, however, are more flexible, or more iconoclastic, or more joyful and rebel at the constraints imposed by mental collection. These individuals not only question, but seek answers as well.

Without postulating a true question, that is, one which seeks a solution, there can be no answers and one will be left stranded amid the digressions of the mortal way. A sincere question, one which captivates one's entire being, will always seek solution. And so, as one asks, so one receives. Questions that posit the ultimate meaning of existence, or the intense need for understanding of God, will be answered on the level they are asked. Some questions are so vast they are not immediately answerable; it may take a lifetime of learning to comprehend the profundity of the solution.

Those who have left behind the safety of the mind, understand the commitment and the dedication necessary to embark upon the road of truth. For truth cannot be taught nor learned, but only experienced. Those who have tasted of truth, are empty without its nourishment. The necessity for truth and for freedom compel one onward, daring the steeper and more treacherous ascents.

The path, then, is an endless movement, one which continually brings the self closer and closer to its own state of knowing. There is no end to this journey and there is no final knowledge. There is, however, that condition when one experiences union with the universe's infinite unfolding of itself. Here, nothing is finished, nor nothing begun, but one no longer seeks; one comes to a state of peace in being consumed by infinity's existence—one is finally free.

Neither a journey nor a direction, but an infinite complexity of Realities, fashioned from the heart of universal longing, is Divine Way. Here exists infinite wisdom, and the creative splendor of life's joy. Here, at the heart of Being, human existence springs forth bejeweled with the very essence of Reality's self. Here in this endless wonder is our human birthright and true home and the yearned for serenity of the One Path, multifarious and unknown.

Illusions

Embarking on freedom's journey requires the dissolution of one's illusory world, because without removing the veils clouding the sight, one is unprepared for the magnitude of divine response. To know the Nameless, one must know the self first—the self in all its trials and pains, the self in its emotions and deceits, the self in its strengths and joys. Pulling illusion from the mind and the heart is one of the most arduous and fearful tasks.

Illusion is historical. It did not begin with one's present state nor spring forth fully grown within one's mind. Illusion remains with humanity, being passed from one generation to the next, giant ancient lineages, each nation, each culture, each family, having its own specific brand of lie. Like immense weights these illusions press into human breast, suffocating the latent sparks and the holy light. Each generation dispels old demons, replacing them with new; and each generation holds dear to its own deceits believing that it alone carries the torch of truth and the one righteousness.

Bred into form, these illusions share intimate knowledge with one's own self. They intermingle with the mind's clear passages and infiltrate the heart; they confuse the psyche and paralyze the intellect. When one is sufficiently infused with illusion, one is finally socialized and ready to partake in human affairs. Some will succumb quickly and remain content in illusion's security. Others fight and struggle, wrenching their hearts and destroying their serenity. Still others refuse the illusion, yet are unable to elude its tenacious grip and suffer life in loneliness. Always, however, in one form or another, one must come to terms with illusion.

Illusion cannot be compromised. It cannot be bought, for the attempt to negotiate with it only strangles one further, deepening illusion's grip upon the heart. No matter when or how one came under illusion's spell, it is always possible to destroy its hold and to forge oneself onto the path of God. To do this, one must first See illusion and out of this sight, one will know what to do.

Illusion is not a thing, nor an evil as one would imagine it to be. It is not corporeal in the sense of inhabiting a specific form, but it is a construction of the mind which inhabits all form and exists in parasitic relationship to the body. The illusion feeds off the body's vital force, its spiritual strength, depleting its store of Light. Illusion breeds within the body's cells infiltrating collective consciousness and yet, it contributes nothing to the well being of that consciousness.

Because of its ubiquitousness and its ancient accumulation upon human journey, man no longer recognizes illusion nor sees it in true form. Illusion is supported by human ignorance and maintained through collective amnesia. Generations and generations of human ancestors suffered its pains and its awful stringent judgments, but still it has not been forbidden to be nourished by mortals.

So closely entwined with human thought has illusion become that individuals do not recognize the psychotic lies it spins nor the grief it dispenses upon life's journey. Here, only humanity can intervene. Illusion comes from human invention and only through human effort can illusion be dispelled. The unreality is so thick, it creates a tangible separation between finite and infinite space and condemns humanity to isolation and aloneness.

Those who bravely walk upon the path to the Unknown will do battle with illusion, slaying the dragons of the mind and cutting nourishment from illusion's parasitic hold. Illusion is just that, unreal. Only the true self, the self that transcends the relative plane has sufficient strength and clear enough sight to face the imposter and destroy it.

To comprehend the nature of illusion, one needs the strength of having experienced what is Real. Illusion is formulated from the human dimension, being an expression of man's first finite wonder, twisted and gone awry. Illusion is named thus for it defines the extent and magnitude of what is unreal. Unreality is tangible and forceful, it can harm as well as lull one into false surrender. As such, illusion shares a paradoxical existence being both physically compelling and ultimately powerless.

Illusion feels real, imposes powerful demands, constrains one's perception of reality, and yet it is not real. Humans inhabit a mirage, a reality of their own creation. Deep within the recesses of collective consciousness grow the seeds of despair and the hopelessness of existence. These seeds germinate through the ages of humanity, sprouting new shoots, cross-pollinating with the many varied fabrications of so many minds. Into the heart of the body, planted on its original descent, goes the illusion of human isolation. And here, on the dusty plains of terror stands the primary deceptor, the desolation and despair.

Doubt clogs the life-blood and diverts one off the path. Doubt instigates confusion and laughs at one's attempt to honor the sacred. Deep into the mind nestles doubt, waiting for one to advance upon an experience of the Other, and then it springs to life questioning one's intention and one's perception. Doubt is a complex reality, illusory, but a reality even so.

To battle doubt, one must see that doubt is not *about* anything. That is, doubt does not arise from its intended object. The condition of doubt germinates from within, where one's very existence is subject to doubt's critical ways. Doubt is not about anything but itself. Doubt is doubt. It does not protect one from falsehoods nor screen out possible illusion. For doubt, not being a reality of its own, can never Act, but only react to its own reflections.

Doubt and despair function together, for who can experience the one without knowing the other? Together they drain the heart and imperil one's ascent along the way. Despair insists that one will never arrive and doubt questions whether there is anywhere to go. Despair debilitates one's energy and feeds off the joyful murmur of infinity's sigh. Reality can do nothing to stop this intrusion, for humans are creators of their own mortal play. And only humans can stop the parasite from feeding upon themselves.

Unworthiness, the feelings of meaninglessness, together with one's doubt and despair fill one's heart and stifle the joy. How can one breathe when such negativity weighs upon the soul? Yet, even this is not sufficient to allay humanity's appetite for self-destruction. Human consciousness is filled with judgment, historical perceptions, cultural decrees, and individual pronouncements upon one's fate. One is no longer free.

Fed from birth, the poor impassioned heart becomes increasingly burdened with humans' illusory way. There is such safety in repetitive ways, in the ritualization of living, and in the smug security of "belonging". It is no wonder that one believes the deception to be real. For surely all this history, this immense accumulation of knowledge, thinkers, poets, artists, prophets, as well as one's very family, community, and nation, cannot be wrong. Surely one does not challenge the fundamental assumption of mortal existence, the acceptance of human sin and unworthiness, the belief in futility and despair.

The path, however, knows of other wisdom and pushes the weary traveler to condemn his own well-being, forcing the mind to see that Reality which is neither conditioned by, nor responsive to, the mortally fashioned one. One may appear self-destructive at this point, or wrongfully led astray. Yet, the Way is neutrally inflexible; if one seeks Truth, one must suffer through the pangs of confusion, fear, and ridicule that necessarily obstruct one's movement.

Nothing can be done to alleviate the intensity of human illness, for piece by piece and section by section the disease of collective amnesia will be stripped from one's consciousness. The disease must be healed and the illusion revealed or one will never come upon that Truth which knows neither of negativity nor deceptive ways.

Here, on the brink of Infinity, one must be willing to challenge all accumulated knowledge, everything, and stand unfettered, as a child, seeking to know the Truth. One must be willing to challenge one's very existence, that existence that is predicated on the assumption of initial sin and that wrestles with the inner heart in silent, forgotten passageways. One must surely want to Know, to drink of Truth, for the desire must be great to sustain the shock and the suffering that will ensue.

Paradoxically, struggle propels one into greater abandonment, allowing the self in moments of freedom to know the Joy that exceeds illusion. One sheds deception for peace and known lies for unknown truth, yet still the body suffers as it passes through the portals of illusion's creation, sobbing for the wasted effort and the terrible amassed history, the toil of the ages, the leaden tears frozen on so many hollowed cheeks, the friendship and the pains, and the loves long forgotten.

But do not fear, for as the heart cries, Infinity washes away illusion's hurt, freeing hatred, and filling the self with Love.

Ego

Powerful as illusion is, more powerful still is the core around which it binds itself to form. Without a core, a self-identified center of being, illusion would be unable to attach to consciousness. Illusion and ego are mutually generating, as the existence of one necessitates the reality of the other.

Ego calls itself by many names, each more subtle than the last. Ego is the essential definition, the first contusion of the mind, wrapped around itself, and jealous of intruders. Ego tenaciously grips its steely place within one's heart, casting out all who refuse its command. Like a spoiled child it attempts to control the formless heart, threatening isolation to those who challenge its reality.

Ego, however, is the real intruder. Attempting to fill the gap between mortality and divinity, the ego develops its own sound. Listening to the voice of no other, ego forms a vacuum within itself. Here, in true isolation, one is left to contemplate the meaning of life and the nature of one's existence.

It is no wonder that humans suffer despair, trapped as they are within a cocoon of their own invention. It is no wonder that they search for answers and relentlessly pound themselves against the very walls of ego's despair. It is no wonder that they cannot hear, for they are prisoners of their own beliefs and narrowed circumspection.

This ego state, this core, is the central point upon which all structures are erected. Without the essential place, the ego, form would not stand. That is, form would be evolving into formless and back again. The ego, however, fixes form, solidifying it into one place, and casts it into identity. Form and ego are simultaneous, and each must have the other to exist.

There are, however, two kinds of ego: the open and the rigid. The open ego knows its purpose is transient and that it serves a higher reality only. It is unafraid to die to itself, for in the dying it knows of other births. The rigid ego, on the other hand, fears for its survival and attaches itself to form with a tenacious grip. This ego attempts to divert anything which might affect its power over form. Closed upon itself, the rigid ego knows of no truth but its own.

These egos roam the planet, wrapping consciousness about themselves. It is not just individuals who suffer from ego's hold, but all creations generated from unsurrendered state. Church and religion, nations and families, thoughts and philosophies, corporations and spiritual groups, all suffer the consequences of ego's ascent into form.

For ego impedes the perception of God directly. It stands between, it serves as the deflector and the judge. It condemns humanity to a life of separation and willful aloneness.

So subtle and unseen is ego's way, that it intertwines with life's most humble pleasures, robbing the self of reality and condemning the heart to self-inflicted imprisonment. What is this ego, then, this compelling digression off divine way?

Who learns to recognize its stance, its often disguised deception, its camouflaged and rigid core beneath the outer frail confusion? This is the task of keen perception, drawn from the depths of one's heart, where the purity remains untainted by ego's guileful way.

To shatter ego's hold, one must be willing to surrender and to stand amid the fears of mortal survival. For ego being ground to form, evokes the deepest uncertainty and challenges each attempt to wrench the demon from one's mind. Confrontations are inevitable now, as one is locked in dire battle with the illusive wretch.

But one must See and Know how ego separates the self from all that is Holy. One must face the pain and the sorrow, and one must study the subtle forms ego takes. For there is no safety from ego's grasp, except in God alone.

Gathering the courage and the sight necessary, one will

begin to recognize the illusion of ego's power. One will understand that nothing in the universe can be owned, and that which is possessed suffocates the owner.

Ego is that place, hidden within form, which tricks one into believing one "belongs". Its core is fear, the fatal loneliness of abandonment, and without the continued sustenance of human endeavor, ego would not stand.

This ego is the most powerful, yet destructible illusion, being intimately wed to material existence. It is the hidden core of all human ills, forming the pattern of deception.

With certainty and surrender, one must spark the eternal Light. For it is only prayer, and the quiet, mysterious holiness that can help one to transcend ego's futile hold.

Survival's Chase

To journey upon the mountains of the Unknown one must be prepared to shed the tenuous and ephemeral human identity. For what is formed by the mind and the social situation is not sufficient to guide one to the divine Presence.

The Truth stands naked and unadorned, and only that which is of the same veracity may glimpse upon the radiant fringes of God's Heart. The very fabric of physical dimension is premised upon human intervention, and so, to come upon the realm of the sacred, one need discard all mortal digressions.

The soul maintains its own identity, yet this division grows outside of egoistic hold. It is the body which learns to collect definitions, gathering the fragments of human idea into a personal collage. From birth the infant self collects the mental pictures which define its very existence and bind it to mortal form. Day by day, the child gathers more and more information, chaining the self to historical recollection and further widening the rift from its Source.

Personality develops, garnered from so many external sources. Mother and father intermingle with friends and relatives, nation and religion, education and intelligence. Each accumulation of information adds to one's personal store, enriching the physical presentation at the expense of the formless holiness.

In this structured reality, there is no room for the unnamed and unknown. For one's very survival now begins to be attached to the development of further identity. Each addition to the mental collection adds to one's security, as name and number, likes and dislikes, fears and other emotions anchor the fluid self.

Drawn deeper and deeper into one's dark psyche, the unspoken traumas gather dust and lay in unconscious array. The hurts and the pains, the memories and the emotions line the inner self, clogging the passageway to Home.

One begins to forget, and dimly wonders about divine state. Slowly one is dying, being tethered to mortal stagnation, as the fear of unknowingness takes hold. It is this fear of nothingness which binds the heart to form, strangling its sacred invention. For here one touches the survival of form, the ultimate illusion of physical dimension.

A prisoner of one's own fears, and suffering the consequences of potential death, one loses sight of the greater whole and succumbs to the illusion. Now one believes that personality exists separate from soul and human psyche can function without the spirit. Here in a realm without wisdom, holiness, or love, one searches for answers to life's problems.

Rooted in fear, the self harbors the pain created by the very same suppressive definition. For without the link to the sacred, one is abandoned and unprotected, one stands alone. Yet the survival of the body exerts such a strong demand upon one's soul, that one loses grounding, often succumbing to the physical command.

One learns to struggle, as if each breath is vital to ward off the battle with death. Each emotion appears precious, no matter how negative, as one begins to be fascinated by life's puzzle. Each definition of the self adds to one's esteem, building the fragile and unrooted personality.

Not only does one collect survival information from the family, but from all of history and mental recollection as well. Drawn upon an ancient lineage, and imbedded into the psyche's nest, stand row upon row of beliefs, myths, remembrances, and truths. Each weighs upon one's ability to stand, untethered and free.

Yet freedom is not survival's concern. For survival attempts to force one to attend to the physical dimension alone. It asserts its authority, citing examples of certain persuasion. For who can deny the fact of mortal death, the decomposition of the flesh?

Time goes by, and one never questions the assumptions nor intentions of this powerful reality. Chained to survival, one lives a life of fear. Afraid to venture forth, afraid to challenge one's assumptions, one exists in a fragmented world.

God cannot enter this abode, for all is uneven and stolen from the residue of antiquity. One must gather courage, and challenge survival's fear, calling forth the death and facing its threat.

One must know death to know life, and one must face the fear to experience freedom. Without discarding the collective definition, one can never arrive at the home of homes, where Infinity resides. For Infinity contains neither definition nor identity, being fashioned by the pillars of Truth, whose magnificence stands outside of form.

Facing death, one will come to know its illusion. For death does not exist upon the sacred planes, but rather is a focus for the mortal stagnation, slowing life's vibration, until the form can no longer imbibe divine sustenance.

Conquering survival's chase, and overpowering its grip upon one's heart, frees the self for exploration, to wander amid the quiet, still voices, calling in the night.

The Call

Weary and worn, the mortal traveler journeys upon the trodden path of human invention. The heart is not stirred nor the passion inflamed any longer by the ancient treadmill. Rituals and roles clog life's vitality, leaving small room for the unordinary and wondrous. Ancient myths weigh upon the human mind, suppressing all but the adventurous and desperate.

Those who survive the giant wheel of history distill a secret longing from life's intent. Not content with processed reality, one questions and yearns to know. So numbed become the senses that the quest takes on an all-important hue. Without it, one fears annihilation, as though one will lose all, succumbing to the hypnotic chant of material existence, and drown in a sea of forgetting.

To ward away the lurking demons of normalcy, one invents the absurd and the fantastic. One creates a world which abides no external reckoning. One demands creativity and sensitive discernment; one refuses the insistent drone of a pre-packaged life.

Somewhere in the rebelliousness rests an intensity and a passion which must be harnassed and used for one's escape to freedom. Somewhere in the depths of one's being lies the very tools needed for the ascent into the Unknown. In some secret way, one knows what to do and one begins blindly and alone, groping in the dark. Somewhere, amidst all the pain, seeds of jubilance are germinating.

Searching begins in earnest now. Never at rest, the soul diligently searches for itself. Frustrated and alone, one begins the unraveling necessary to sort out the fabric of the insane. So many intertwined realities impinge upon one's very existence, so many frozen and clogged passageways obstruct one's communion with higher states, one feels helpless and incapable of further advancement.

Down into the abyss of despair one sinks, convinced of mortal error. Gone is the certainty, the assurance, and the willful quest. Gone is the knowledge of what to do, and gone is the desire to get there. Surrendering to the mind's deception proves fatal, for one is lost in a mire of illusion.

One falls further and further down, down to the bottom, where one can no longer fall. Here, one is forced to surrender all. Everything. The fear of normalcy, karma, and pain; the fear of judgment, annihilation and starvation; the fear of ultimate evil and personal sin.

Darkness descends upon the heart.

Nothing is heard for some time to come.

Eons may pass, yet it may be but a moment. In the surrendered nothingness, a still voice beckons the weary aspirant and instills the passion of forgetfulness, into human breast. "Come," calls the voice, "come, for I am near."

Arisen from mortal subjugation, one learns to heed the quiet voice of Love. Following the mystical call, one confronts the immense reality without name. Summoned by divine intent, the heart sheds the self-same fears of human illusion.

The Call beckons the traveler to its melodious sound, basking the soul in divine light. The self thirsts for the mysterious harmony and yearns for the whisper of God's name. The Call becomes everything, consuming one's being in its magnificent resonance, and reflects the fabric of one's very existence.

Yet the self still struggles between the world of the prosaic and the majestic, battling the force of the material plane. Desirous of God's way but still attached to earthly soil, one is torn by the fact of physical existence.

The Call, however, is intimately entwined with human life, being the divine dimension of light. Infiltrating the essential fibers of Being, the calling is God's song and latent command within human breast. Great harmonious oneness enjoins divine intent, radiating into form and back again, and wraps all creation in the Call's multifarious symphonies.

Despite the pain and the divergent struggles, the divine beckoning exerts a profound presence within human consciousness and binds the self to its whispered jubilance. One knows God is within; one hears the silent melody and glimpses the hems of peace. One must endure the tribulations, for only in the assignation with negativity can one develop the strength to unceasingly follow the soul's Call.

Here one enters an interior world, a world inhabited by mystical possibilities and sacred wisdoms. Here upon the fathomless meadows of splendor, the soul enjoins the eternal call to divine breast and partakes in the sound of silence.

One becomes God's beckoning, being both the beckoning and the called. Never separate from the soul's search for its home, the Call directs the wayless self amidst the meaning and the purpose of sacred life.

Blessed now by Love's sounds, one advances tenuously along the steep and rocky crevices, reaching for the balance of God's Call, and knowing that one's ascent is compelled by creation's yearning for itself.

For what more could stir the heart than the sound of the eternal Voice?

Abandoned Self

When all is still and night descends upon the soul, the heart yearns for love's serene abandonment. In the darkened, solitary night, where no mortal eye beholds, the worldly shell unravels, exposing layer upon layer of human image. Stepping outside of time, the heart lays down its fears of ultimate nakedness and awaits the holy embrace.

Like useless weapons the human defenses are lain upon the soil of Love, revealing the jewels of vulnerability. Pride, arrogance, and shame rest side by side with fear, anguish, and despair. Jealousy, hate, and ego are melted in the living flame. And the pillars of identity fall, tumbling upon the eons of antiquity, crumbling all of human history in their wake.

Without name, without home, without profession or relation stands the revealed soul, unclothed and blameless in the night. Devoid of thought, idea, or prayer, the heart prepares for its moment of Being. Stripped of all world attachments, the soul rests upon the endless sheets of light, vulnerable and unknown.

Alone, yet united, confined, yet free, the self is shattered by the dismantling of structures, the security of the mortal plane. Structure upon structure must go, taken apart within the mighty fury of divine essence. Every possession, every tangible crutch will be destroyed by the Light. All fascination with power and all attachment to form will yield to the overwhelming Love.

Devotion to structure and form is not sufficient to bring one to the holy doorstep. Only in the vulnerable state of Being can one unite with that which stands outside of creation. For encased within ethereal body are multitudes of historical thoughts. The hopes and fears, the myths and fantasies, and the sorrows and joys of the human family. All image must be shed for Love.

Into the arms of Love, one will discard the shields, the generations of thought and social history. Scattered upon the plains of eternity, the mortal wounds heal as the soul confronts its own presence. Empty of image, and free of historical constraint, the heart will burst open, discarding the needless shell of human protection.

All is nothing compared to the Love. Prophets and deities, masters and knowledge, holy incantations and profound art, are mere images of All that Is. To cleave unto the mortal, no matter how compelling, is to insert external structures between oneself and God. For only in complete abandonment of image, in total dismantling of the self, can one experience God directly.

Nothing can be owned in this realm of the sacred. For nothing is needed. In the total abandonment of self identification, one embraces infinity Itself.

Oh, splendid, unfettered self! All is and is not. Both surrendered and distinct, one is now Home.

Exquisite vulnerability and gentle passion of divine intent open the secret tabernacle of the heart's awakening. Miraculous existence, joy of joys, here in the nothingness one finds the true meaning.

Without image, without identity, and free of mortal definition, the naked self stands revealed. Empty yet full, this is the self of divine way. Identified by the beams of love and the shimmering silver lights, this self needs nothing other than its birthright in God.

The abandoned self stands outside of history, without anchors to the physical plane. It no longer searches for a home among the ruins of the mortal way. It ceases to yearn for the temporal delight, knowing another Love. All human image holds no sway upon this unchained self and never again will direct its movement.

In the tabernacle of the Heart, one is simultaneously nothing and All that Is. Shedding the eons of definition, the abandoned self finally becomes itself, mystery within mystery, Holiness made manifest.

Now truly itself, the self moves within another sphere. Abandoned and in union, the soul awaits the passion of divine embrace. Never again to suffer aloneness nor abandonment, the heart journeys upon the multitudinous rays of wisdom, imbibing Love.

Great lessons are instilled, imprinted within the heart's very beat. Infused with God's image, the self evolves along eternity's path, experiencing the sacrament.

Forever abandoned, seeking nothing but God's grace, one soars within the holy freedom, life within life, majestic castles of deliverance, and entrusts the self to Love.

Ascent to the Unknown

Fortified with spiritual strength and firmly upon the path of divine yearning, one begins the ascent in God's way, forging a solitary trail up the mountains of deception and through the valleys of the void, with neither marker nor guide, in darkness, amid the Unknown.

Here, one is left to contemplate, for only in the still darkness can one come to know that which has no name. The contemplation infuses the Self with God's existence, being the core of All That Is. Only in the quiet, unseen night, may one be filled with this wondrous Splendor and set upon the sea of divine unfolding.

More than a word, more than a sight, this darkness is Everything, the primordial seed, the cosmic essence, so full of Itself, it cannot manifest. Inside, yet outside, one and the same, God involutes upon the Self. Deeper and deeper into the recesses of one's being is one drawn. Darker and darker are the passageways; no light shines forth; no sound beckons one's attention. One is left with the stark mystery of the Unknown.

Groping in the dark, witness to unfathomable truths, the soul gathers strength. One still cannot see, but sight is not important now. All that is important is given. Immense waves of darkness consume one's very being, shaking the foundations of mortal image, deed, and thought, and leaving the self stripped of all physical support.

Now one must confront the mortal way, the illusive deceptions, and the graven images which stand between oneself and God. Nothing is left unturned; the smallest deceit magnifies within the darkness, calling forth the judgment, which is Self confronting self. For nothing can remain in the Holiness. All obstructions, all falsehoods, negativities, and unclean emotions will be distilled from the heart amid the dark and infinite Nameless.

The myriad facets of ego will be shattered, to be replaced by divine surrender. The arrogance of the mortal way will be melted in the fire of Humility; and the incessant, agitated thought stilled by the hand of Love.

The darkness cannot be seen nor identified; it responds to

no claim other than God's own. It is immovable and absolute; one cannot leave at will nor attempt to name its endless realities. It descends upon one's soul, enveloping every crevice of one's being, and leaves one mute, without reprieve.

Cries for release are of no use; no one can hear. One is alone, solitary and confined, within the blameless judgment, scouring out the insides of one's soul and mending the initial separation from God's Heart.

It is the separation that rends mortal pain, most potent lie of form. Into the tunnels of loneliness and despair, and upon the barren plains of sin and mortal error, one must crawl. Face to face with this terrible suffering, this first, unnecessary, severance from infinite Being. Waves of grief consume the soul, breaking one's heart, and revealing the wound in consciousness.

Closer and closer one is drawn into the first pain, the cosmic agony over separation of Self. There is no escape. One is dragged into the pits of desolation and the prideful denial of despair. One is scorched upon the arrogant dismissal and the fateful, sorrowful aloneness. And in the darkness, one knows Reality, amid the endless wail, humanity's cry for Home.

Out of this nameless suffering compassion grows, sprouting flowers of love whose fragrance intoxicates the mortal shell and resuscitates the weakened heart. Upon the momentary surrender, separation no longer exists and one is embraced by infinite Grace.

Back and forth in darkness one will wander for some time to come. Moments of understanding and love will coexist with episodes of intense waylessness and despair. All will be lost, one will know the nothingness, and stand in fear of ultimate annihilation. But always in the darkness one is guided by the unseen hand of Love.

The Love may be brutal, it may desolate the soul; yet always it anoints the heart, marking the next ascent along infinity's splendorous path.

One must be in darkness to See, and in silence to Hear. One must be surrendered to know the workings of Divinity. Within surrender is born the newness and the atunement to divine heartbeat. For only in complete abandonment of the world's way can mortal heart be rewoven into the fabric of God's Self, never to suffer aloneness again.

Surrender exacts a steep price from the mind's illusion. It causes all images to quake within the infinite darkness. Surrender yanks out the roots of separation, removing the superficial selves from the structural layers of reality, and casting them into the cleansing fires. For only when one is without external image, when one ceases to grasp for defensive shield, is one able to withstand the exquisite surrender, and be healed in the timeless Love.

Climbing ever onward, the solitary journeyer comes to know the unspeakable and powerful fortitude of darkness. Each ascent replenishes the vital spiritual passageways and mends a segment of human separation from the Divine. Each victory over one's demons reveals greater truths unspoken and brings one closer to sacred intent.

The darkness is the meaning of Light wherein one will find the holy, living Truth.

Although darkness shrouds the soul, this is not the darkness of ignorance nor evil ways. This is the darkness of the Light, the Immensity which remains unarticulated within mortal breast. For all is dark and unknown, until one is sufficiently free of human image to withstand the Divine Light.

This infinite darkness is full, it teems with God's myriad realities. From the depths of the silence emanates the Word, and from the unseen Immensity springs forth creation itself. Here, in the unspeakable, resides the holy intonations and the ancient, melodious mysteries; here one studies the Unnamed and the Unknown.

The darkness, then, is the condensed expression, the holiness unmanifest. It is the Source of All that Is. The darkness is a friend and wordless teacher. To come out of darkness, one must mend the mortal separation from divine Being, for only in union can the heart manifest and create.

Light is created out of darkness being the first expression of the unnamed holiness. Each union of the self in God brings one into greater creative oneness wherein all holy mysteries abide. Here one becomes that which is sought. Here wisdom infuses the soul.

As the union increases and one grows closer to the heart of darkness, beyond the first, fateful separation, one begins to Know and to See. Now one is able to tentatively speak. Like an infant learning the native tongue, the spiritual seeker slowly and arduously forms the language of God.

Letter by letter and word by word, one begins to comprehend the vocabulary of Love and the magnificent, sacred sentences. Paragraphs of wisdom live, interwoven in the endless volumes of God's splendor. Each letter, each word, touches the very core of one's existence, resonating into sound and spilling over into form. One speaks, and one begins the journey from darkness into light.

Back and forth one goes, captivated by Divine Grace. Each utterance of human breath reflects upon the holiness and brings one closer to the Unknown. Back and forth, from the unmanifest to the manifest, one journeys, echoing the pattern of life.

It is within the depths of the dark contemplation that the self comes to know the divinity of its nature. It is the solitary ascent which prepares the soul for its entrance into the light. And it is the confrontation with illusion which distinguishes the transitory from the real.

As one is cleansed of human frailties and freed from the chains of mortal despair, the soul is drawn closer and closer to its Source. The mortal pain of separation is replaced in union as one collapses into the arms of God. Never to be alone again, one embarks on the ultimate ascent—fusion with the Unknown.

The Unknown, vast infinite storehouse of divinity, presses into one's very being pushing out all exterior thought. In this uncharted territory there is no guide except God alone and no beacon save the heart's compelling passion. God and self join in One, no separation exists, and the soul is stamped with Infinity's grace.

At this point, mortal individualism ends as one joins within God's self-same Image. The two, yet one, remain forever re-united. Home of homes and final resting place, one now witnesses the profundity of divine Love.

Unknown only to mortal mind, this place is infinity Itself, never-ending and composed of Joy. Into the enveloping Love one is drawn, to learn the Way of the Infinite and the Process of Divinity. For never, in ceaseless time, can one Articulate All that Is.

The journey is forever, the ascent appears alternately formidable and simple as one struggles along the pathways of moral limit. God is a continual movement, an infinity of realities, endless wisdom, edifices of Joy. Nothing manifested approximates the Unknown.

As one is purified, the self becomes this Truth. In fragments and in snatches, at times of love and in moments of surrender, one grows more and more like God. Building moment by moment, in quiet contemplation, the heart learns the Immensity of divine emotion.

Only in the still, untouched tabernacle can one learn the Unknown Way. Separate from historical voice and social identification, divine guidance will mark the path. Without physical proofs and mental evidence, the heart will be blessed with Trust.

Ever more into God's Heart, surrendered on eternity's wings, the self arrives at the One home, sharing in the splendor of the Unknown.

The Language of Love

Here in the Sanctuary, at rest in the Unknown, Love coalesces in divine contemplation and breathes life upon the nothingness. Love, first principle of creation, infuses the formless with the structural equations of God's mansions, and causes the multifarious and unmanifested life to partake of dimension.

Leaving the infinite freedom, and beckoned by divine Will, the formless balances between the passive and the active pendulums, and becomes fixed upon a particular dimensional home. It is the Love which serves as catalyst, igniting the unknown emptiness, and spewing forth creation.

It is the Love which embodies the divine Emotions and channels Them into the many-hued forms. Each creation different, yet the Same, unravels within the mighty holy breath. And form, the first sustenance of God's manifestation, being all One and holy and fashioned from its unknown self, stands erected by the power of grace.

Form contains the very essence of eternity, for otherwise Love would not be able to condense the nothingness into manifested life. Form itself is woven within the tabernacle of divine Heart, and shares the fabric of infinity upon its breast.

It is the language of Love which beckons the unknown darkness into the garment of manifested state. It is the language of Love which bestows the very essence of divine Word, enflaming the passive being into creative life. And it is the language of Love which breathes existence, moment by moment, sustaining the unmanifested holiness into form.

What of this Love, prime mover, and bridge between Being and creation? What of this latent Mystery, profoundly imprinted within human breast? What of this Language, unspoken, yet known, deep within the recesses of creation's self? What Word calls the majestic soul into life's wheel and sets the ancient Memory into mortal mind?

What of this Love?

Word unmanifest, unspoken, Love fills the fabric of creation. Cascading waters of God's Heart, Love pours into form, nourishing the smallest fibers of Being. Bejeweled rainbow, Love embodies the great Wisdoms and reveals the Mysteries silently housed within the Unknown.

From the unmanifest nothingness and upon the bridge of formation, Love aligns the infinite Being, bringing God into form. Intense inward volition, Love spawns creation's self. Love springs forth from the void, being one with the Unknown, sounding the nameless incantation. Yet able to sacrifice, Love comes out of itself, journeying upon the many beams of Light and coalescing into dimensions.

In its outward journey Love carries with It the mansions of infinity's Heart. Humility, honor, and grace join creation with devotion, compassion, and strength. Laughter, joy, and humor intermingle with yearning and passion. Each aspect of the eternal Unknown is drawn upon Love's wings and instilled within the silent resting place of the soul.

Infinity's mansions unfold, multi-faceted and unknown. Sparkles of Being radiate out through God, and are breathed upon life by Love's eternal grace. Here each sound is anointed from above and reflects the holiness of All that Is. Into form Love journeys, carrying a unique configuration of God's self.

The letters of Emotion are married to the numerals of the Law, giving birth to divine equations, first form. Each letter reflects a divine reality, exquisite and eternal bliss. And the Law dictates how many of each, and in which dimensions, shall the letters be drawn. Yet it is the Love which binds the two and fuses them into Word, both splendorous and forgotten.

The Word resonates within space, beckoning the condition of existence. Beyond time does Word enjoin Word, building God's stories. Multi-dimensional, neither up nor down, living sentences are constructed, the language of Love is born.

Each creation unique, being formed from the self-same properties of God, contains its own special combination of divine Emotions. Here the unmoving nameless rests at the center of the soul's unfolding, continuously recollecting the pattern of divine birth. Pulsating paragraphs of joy, creation becomes manifested.

Without this language of Love, form could not manifest, nor God be born through mortal existence. Infinite Being, creating and non-creating on one, radiates bliss, blessing all that is.

Bejeweled creation, self-same reflection of divine right, echoes the language of Love. Within the secret passageway mortal heart holds the key which unlocks the ancient mystery of God and man as one.

Yet only the Love can guide the self upon this divine journey, only the Love can unravel the multitudinous equations and bring the heart into Knowing.

Within the eternal dimensions of Joy, Love journeys forth carrying the sacred passages. Each holy Word gathers Others to Itself and coalescing in divine proportion catapults through Time, and joins dimension.

This sacred jewel, multiple facet of God's heart, glistens between realities, becoming soul, complex harmony and sacred paragraph in God. Child of Being's own Self, never separate, but of One Substance, the soul pulsates with divine Love.

Through the window of the heart, deeper into the vocabulary of divinity, one joins the infinite realities of God. Never at end, existence breathed in and out, from the heart of Being. Here the self studies the myriad Truths, comprehended by the heart alone.

Splendorous Truths, builder of creations, riding forth on the beams of Love! Endless search which leads one out and back again from the farthest reaches into the very mortal heart, seeking all one and the same Truth. Great mystery of existence resides within mortal breast wherein one finds the pathway upon divinity's own self.

Speaking to none but the Heart alone, the Love stirs divine recollection, calling forth the inner seed, nestled within human breast. For Being has no name and hears none other than Itself.

Only the simple and the humble hear the majestic symphonies and gaze upon the many-dimensional edifices of Love. Here one witnesses the magnificent Emotions, divine couriers, leading the chariots of Truth. Here one is transfixed by the Law and restructured, so that all sin falls.

Love weaves infinity's longing into form, gathering divine Emotions and setting them upon the fabric of the soul. Endlessly rich, each Emotion embodies a reality of Infinity's own self and ushers one into the realm of Truth. For each facet of Emotion one comes to know, only serves to uncover the next, more profound reality, still.

Awesome in scope and never-ending, these Emotions render one speechless. Far more beautiful than anything of created dimension, these Emotions reveal the wonder and majesty of Truth. They are the food of the spirit and the nourishment for creation, without which existence could not be.

There is such joy in the infinite wisdom! Layer and layer upon itself, deeper and deeper one can learn, never to arrive at a final solution. Love, honor, humility, grace, tenderness, and compassion, grow upon each soul, and never, in endless time, can one comprehend the myriad wisdom of each.

Never will one be able to hold the truth of divinity itself, nor to possess it through willful means. Only may one increasingly come to experience and be the Emotion, the Love made manifest. As one sheds the divisions of the mind and the temptations of the flesh, one begins to wander amid the pillars of Love. Each act of unselfishness and every attempt at transcendent understanding, will help to align the physical presence with the Divine.

As the body trains itself to respond to the higher instincts and to discard the baser human emotions, the soul positions itself into communion with the mortal self. As one disbands with the ephemeral human response, the way of reaction and fear, the soul instills insight into the heart and directs the action along the course of another way.

To replace fear with love and anger with compassion, one will experience the meaning of wisdom. As each human weakness is eliminated, the language of Love becomes known. Only in the silent recesses of the heart can one discern the immensity of divine Love. For each small sacrifice is sufficient to enable the heart to behold the grace and infinite wisdom of Being.

Gliding on the planes of divinity, one traverses the facets of Emotion and discovers exquisite splendor in the Unknown. The essence of all life exists here and the strength that is the true sustenance resides within the mansions of Truth. The passion for Truth stirs one onward and fans the curiosity bounded to existence.

This is the language of Love, eternal communicator of Truth. Following the letters and the words of Emotion, learning to speak the simple sentences of Wisdom, one comes slowly to embrace the divine passion and to rejoin the fabric of God.

Mystical Heart

Oh Heart of splendor, Heart which knows no separation from All that Is. This is the majestic resurrection of suffering wherein all wounds are mended and divine grace infuses the self.

On the flowered pastures of Being, this Heart blazes in radiant light, emanating the mysterious Sweetness of creation and infusing existence with Love.

So profoundly beautiful is this state, that a glance upon it purifies the vilest error. Nothing can demean this Heart, nor cause blemish upon its unparalleled splendor.

Emotions pour forth from its center, great wisdoms and divine attributes, coalescing in combinations and affixed into form. Such joy abounds, nothing but devotion sounds. Only surrender and humility guide the hearts home.

There is only joy and love, beauty and peace. There is only music and nothing more. Radiating out, blinding light, realities of God fill space. Nothing is needed. All stand naked and vulnerable to be clothed by the infinite Grace.

The mortal heart is pierced by the intense Presence and transformed into holiness. All is restructured by the profound beingness of Love. Love is Itself and nothing more, being the first guiding principle of creation.

And emanating from Its center, cascading symphonies of color, flow blinding Lights, condensed intensity of Love. Lasers of God, separating the moral from the infinite, holy Words enjoined by sacred call. Filtering into the nothingness, Mystical Heart radiates Power.

Silent abundance stills the night and teaches creation of holy ways. Instructed by the beams of eternity, life is infused with Mystery. This Heart, filled with compassion and exploding capsules of bliss, rains communion upon us all.

Oh Holiness, oh sacred Love, fill the multitudinous heavens with Love's fragrance and intoxicate creation in whose sphere thou art embraced.

Dimensions of the Soul

The Love reveals the reality where no judgment takes hold and showers the aspirant with welcomed respite from human sin. It is the Love which teaches one the Truth of surrender and instills the balm of divine Grace.

Love, then, is the shield and the warrior, and the mighty fortitude which prepares the self to conquer the inner demons. Love strengthens the mortal shell and heals the wounds exposed by life's struggles. And Love serves as the necessary understanding which prepares the heart to witness the soul's dimensions.

For it is the soul, manifestation of divine Truth, which embodies the many-faceted levels of Love. The soul, higher form of mortal self, neither bounded to nor touched by fate, radiates divine Emotions from the heart of God.

Here in the many mansions of the soul one shall wander upon Grace and be stricken with God's majesty. Here the quiet, still darkness resides and the melodious harmony resonates. The soul is the holy platform upon which one must tread to journey into greater dimensions still. For one must know the higher form of self to know the higher forms of God and to then comprehend the unknown.

The soul is multi-dimensional and simultaneously exists in multiple time. Each soul, being a spark of greater soul still and intricately set amid the jeweled necklace of a greater Plan, embodies a particular configuration of divinity. Yet each manifests its lessons in perfect proportion and alone solves the riddle of mortal birth.

Upon the outer fringes of the soul's being accumulate the numerous errors of the mortal plane. Here each being's karma is attracted to the soul's external mantle and renders cause and effect upon the glimmering lights attaching human body to spiritual form.

For each unresolved cause on the mortal plane, a cosmic effect is transmitted to the soul's mantle, solidifying the exterior walls and freezing the divine heartbeat. This is the wheel of life, the attachment to earthly plane, and this is the first plateau of resolution where the human and divine self shall meet.

Until one unravels and removes the effects obstructing entrance to the soul, one cannot know freedom. One must return to the first cause and rectify the error in all times simultaneously and in the present space to begin the process of discernment. Only when this task is completed and one knows the nature of mortal error, may one proceed along the multi-jeweled planes, home of the self.

In the soul is stored the Memory, the masterful recollection of all one's lives and the lessons and evolution of each. Each soul houses its memory in distinct ways, some in crystals, others in poetic volumes, and still others in formless sounds. The method is not significant, only the ability to call forth the Memory is what remains.

Hearts of purity may beckon forth the Memory, and reminisce, playfully tumbling through the eons of Time. To those without blemish the Memory affords joy and solace and traverses both in dreams and in the waking state, knowing no bounds. To those who violate the unwritten Law and tamper with the eternal Word, Memory grips the heart with an unspeakable terror and compels the judgment of Self upon self.

Once again one witnesses what is given. To some the outer facets of the soul bring solace while to others, terror. Yet, the soul is neither fixed nor thing, but living, changing Reality, blessed by Holy Breath and birthed by divine Light.

Into the dimensions of the soul one may wander as each wisdom is absorbed and each truth observed. Interior dimensions are revealed with each successive accomplishment as one partakes of the mystery of the self. Exquisite and unique arrangement, the soul is an edifice to Love.

Composed of God's own self, each divine creation embodies miraculous equations, the children of Emotion and Law. Splendorous lights, wisdom abounds, and no word is spoken. This is the realm of Experience, where mortal form confronts the divine soul and where union rifts all barriers asunder.

Now silently within the mansions of the soul, one perceives the echo of infinity. Encapsulated divinity, the soul is both one and separate within God's Heart. Journeying within the soul's dimensions one discovers the endless and unutterable Truth. Never to be understood, it is but the heart which comprehends the Immensity.

Facets within facets, God's reflection everywhere, the soul a structure built by the very elements of divine Self. Bricks of devotion hold up the temple of Truth, shielding the tabernacle of Mysteries. A river of surrender flows into the waterfall of compassion, stirring the sea of splendor upon divine reflection.

Flowers bloom aside the banks of Love's passage and laughter takes flight into the perfumed air of divine night. The winds of strength fan the fire of passion, calling forth the chariots of Emotion. In pairs they come, pulling the pillars of Light, circling round in holy contemplation.

Joyous procession, led by Love, adorns the avenues of Humility, and winds its way into the sacred and mysterious Heart. Anointed and untouched, most beautiful Heart radiates bliss, illuminating all the dimensions with Love.

Beckoned by the Heart and transfixed by the Light one is absorbed into the eternal soul. Resting within the silence, cushioned by the wondrous joy, one sheds distinction and is no longer alone.

It is here, in the Mystery, that one becomes the eternal Image. It is here, where the Unknown anchors itself to form, that the self is discarded to begin the journey of Union, beyond the dimensions of the soul, beyond that which can be spoken.

The Absolute

Arriving at the home of Being's Self one faces the essential construction of creation. For now one stands face to face with the Law and the immutable divine Emotions.

The universe unfolds, unending, fashioned from the properties of divine Heart, always in movement, yet always the same, nothing is drawn that is not of the Holy Self. The Truth is flexible, mutable, and changing as well as firm, immutable, and fixed. And all creation manifests from this self-same State.

It is this Truth which houses the Law and Emotion, and translates the Infinite into finite dimension. Yet the Truth remains the same, subdividing the great mysteries to match its function in form. From the smallest particle to the greatest endeavor, the principle is all One and the Same, as the universal mystery binds creation to Itself.

Here one comes upon the realm of the Absolute, where there is only Truth and no exception. The Truth stands in mighty corridors, illuminated from within, and fuses with the act of creation until the Holy Light sustains each structure upon dimensions. Infusing creation with the equations of the Law and the letters of Emotion.

All Holy Light, great power radiates Truth upon all spheres, closing the circle unto Being's Self. There is no other reality save that of the Truth, which emits its miraculous Being upon the intonations of the heavens. All One and the Same.

Just as water maintains its identity through the equation of its form, so too does all creation exist through the structural purity of Truth. Without this Truth there would be no existence, as each reflects the subdivision of divinity's Self.

In the face of the Absolute, all ego falls as each self is humbled by the immensity of beauty. Washed in the waters of surrender, one partakes of eternal wisdom and learns to shed the allegories of the physical plane. For there is not relative truth, nor myriad interpretations of this state, but only one Absolute, multifarious and incomprehensible, filling the heavens.

Yet Truth cannot be consumed nor possessed. It cannot be held within the framework of the mortal mind, nor be comprehended by a rigid heart. The Truth cannot enter where a lie is beheld, neither can it illuminate those who willfully exclude its estate. Truth exists and forms the very structure of one's existence. Truth pulses into form, coursing through one's spiritual veins, and sustains the holy life.

One may choose to ignore Truth, or to deny the inevitability of its power. One may stand amid error or create new systems to justify human disease. Truth, however, remains the Same. It is immutable to anything of lesser state. For although Truth encompasses all existence, it resonates with nothing other than Itself. Neither sin and evil, illusion and despair, intellectual constructions, nor denial and fear, can know the miraculous mansions of Truth.

It is only the surrendered heart and the divine mind that have the capacity to comprehend the immense wisdom and profound beauty which sustain All that Is. For it is Love which forms the gateway to the Absolute and upon whose wings the self will soar to the heights of divine ecstasy.

The Absolute is home and seat of eternal security. Upon the principles of Truth, along with the precise prisms of the Law, and through the enraptured domains of Emotion, one joins the cosmic serenity. Here the Truth is known, and all falsehoods are shed as the ages of misconception are melted by the power of Love. Mortal temptations dissolve as the soul divulges its transgressions, and the self joins the home of peace where one is finally cleansed of error.

Truth is revealed as one steps outside of mortal lie and learns to know oneself. Plowing through the clogged passages of temporal life, and wielding the sword of intention, one will confront the limited, human truth. This segregated truth is painful, as it is fashioned from mortal will. Yet it must be perceived to redeem one's heart from the stranglehold of humanity.

Through the systems of truth one will move, discarding the rules and regulations, the sins and moral constructs, and all other restrictions instigated by the human will. Tethered to the illusions of the social plane, one will sift through and evaluate the numerous levels of judgment which enforce barriers between oneself and divine knowledge.

Until one suffers through the fires of human illusion, one will be unable to discern the Real from the relative, and the Divine from the temporal. One must know the mortal self, with all one's pains, deceptions, and despairs, to know one's greater self and to pass through the portals of Paradise.

This Truth cannot be taught, nor divine discernment learned, but only in the silent trust and faith may one advance to the dwelling place of divine mind. Here one will come to Know, for hidden beneath the confusion of mortal life rests the unnamed and holy Pattern. Calling forth the passion of remembrance, one must search without respite until the heart begins to resonate the divine beat. Knowing no answer exists within the mortal sphere, the elevated mind seeks solution in the libraries of Truth.

All one's senses come to rest, as one joins in the sacred study, imbibing wisdom. Now nothing from the mortal plane disturbs the impassioned search, as one stands alone amid the quiet, unseen Truth. Transformed by the very nature of oneself, one yearns to remain in the Absolute.

Forever one may study the sacred wisdoms and wander among the multiple dimensions of Truth. Eternally will grow one's love of Truth and one's awe in Its unfoldment. All one's passion will flow with the divine Emotion, filling the heart with ecstasy, as one witnesses the miraculous precision of the Law. One becomes the Peace as the self is abandoned to the Absolute, the one and only Reality.

Never again shall one fear, as one reunites with the eternal Pattern.

Union

Now adorned with majestic beauty, abandoned to Love's way, and into the eternal embrace shall one be called. Joined together with all Holiness and breathed through with divine Grace, one becomes fused with the Unknown.

The mind stands still and harbors neither thought nor action, relinquishing control to the heart. Into another realm the self is drawn, where All emerges, yet without beginning. To comprehend this magic place, one must trust with passion and dispense with doubt, despair, and all logical sequences of the mind. Here is the abode of wisdom, where Truth is Known and needs no verifier.

Cause and effect hang in the balance of Time and leave no trace upon divine way. For here, in Union, separation does not exist, and so from whence could cause arise? Without initiator, effect remains empty as well, here in the abode of Being. There is only pure Being, and action without reaction, that leaves no trace within the heavens.

Union Is Love, beyond mentioning. Love knows only of Itself, being untouched by anything that is not of Same. Hence, nothing can be forgiven, for nothing exists of erroneous nature, here in the Perfection.

Upon the divine dimensions of Being, the magnitude of beauty pierces the heart and shocks the perceptual consciousness. In the heights of Sacred knowledge, and in the rarified atmosphere of Love, not one fragment of mortal image takes hold. There is nothing but eternity and majesty in this dwelling place of Joy.

Union radiates compassion, where neither I nor Thou evolves, but only the self-same reflection of God's estate. Opposites cannot root here in infinity, for there must exist form and definition to create that which is opposed. But in Union, form cannot solidify, remaining fluid and changing, formless to form and back again.

Dualisms cannot grow, neither doubt, cynicism, nor despair. For what one Is knows not separation. This is another order of Reality, one where judgment, decision, skepticism, proof, and other forms of mortal security have no meaning.

Right and wrong, good and evil, moral decisions, and all

other divisions of the mind take no hold upon the divine Union. For all is loved, and holy grace, without blemish nor mistaken identity.

Union is the state where one knows life is of the same fabric, woven from the heart of Being, and fashioned into form. The abundant strength and the delicate gentleness call the same Source home. The smallest particle and the most majestic mountain emerge from within Union's whole. The great prophet and the frail sinner are loved and sustained by the same Breath.

All is of One, yet teeming with diversity. Like one immense, multi-dimensional, unfathomable organism, the universe unfolds. The Center is everywhere, connecting all aspects to Itself. There is nothing that is not joined within the dynamic, radiant Heart.

The slightest offense resonates to the Center, affecting all creation in its pain. For all is One, joined in grace. Yet, also, each expression of compassion and act of goodness fills creation with Love. It is folly to think that one exists isolated and alone, for all thoughts and actions become intimately intwined with divine Self.

From the dimensions of Union arise action, the pure expression of creation's Being. This action is not separate from Union, but enacts the meaning of the whole. In perfect timing and always in balance, holy action is drawn to its need, mending and filling those aspects that are worn, and changing others into new form.

Drawn from the center of divinity, action erupts into space, healing all that is wounded and restoring the integrity of creation. New aspects will be designed and other dimensions invented, but always action is directed to the sustenance of the whole.

Being born of Union, one is never separate from the fate of the whole, riding on the crests of eternity and nestled into divine breast. There is nothing to be done, nor anything to prove, for one exists within the very framework of life, All.

It is Union which bestows serenity, drawing one upon the mantle of divine embrace. Comingling with great mystic Heart, one beholds the surrender of infinite Love. Here in the Union, no faith need abide for no faith is needed, as one is fused with sacred Being.

Mighty power abounds, radiating condensed Light upon all spheres. Melted by the intensity of Being, one ceases to exist, merging beyond separateness. Holy surrender, life has no limit, infusing all with extraordinary beauty.

Faith nor hope are unneeded here, for all is bliss, and already exists in divinity's grace. Miraculous Being, beyond imagining, IS. Never in need again, nor alone, one joins the cosmic laughter, and sits upon the throne of Joy.

Joy

Oh laughter, oh ecstasy, beauty overflows the prisms of divine Being! Exploring the sacred crystals, one is illuminated by rainbows of Joy. Droplets of bliss rain upon one's heart, opening the tabernacles of mystery and releasing one's love anew.

All is refreshed and cleansed within Joy's powerful dwelling place, as the soul is infused with the white, rainbow Light. Following the spectrum of dimensions, the Joy instills humor into mortal breast, igniting the cosmic jester, an imprint of divine plan.

Oblivious to mortal ways, Joy ventures on, neither touched nor affected by negativity's hold. Magnificent brilliance, Joy flames the dark night, calling forth the demons from their hiding places. Turning the intense passion of itself upon all creation, Joy ferrets out the digressors, bringing them home through the Light.

Nothing can be hidden from the Joyful intensity, as it gathers to itself the weakened and the worn and restores the abused to its rightful place. Fear is melted by the Joyful exuberance and worldly concerns cannot mark the mantle of this wondrous State.

For time and history, evil and wrongdoing, error and judgment, cannot trample nor defile the Joy, as it bursts upon all creation, sparkling in the night. If but one could remain within the Joyful serenity, the moral illusion would crumble, revealing all Sacredness in its wake.

Distilled upon Eternity, Joy blesses existence, filling one's cells with the perfume of its way. Oh Holy sustainer, Joy nourishes the emergent souls, filling them with jubilance.

Joy's fragrance perfumes the heavens, rendering all creation delirious with love. No words can describe this state, where one is filled with cosmic laughter, bursting from excitement, and intoxicated with divine bliss.

Oh happiness, and peaceful surrender, all is well and untouched. The universe stands unharmed, ultimately fortified, as the radiant and powerful Joy anchors existence to the great, melodious Heart.

Abandoned, the heart hears another way, elevating consciousness to another plane. In Joy, all needs are forgotten and all trials dissolved, for God is at home, resplendent in the Unknown.

Hear not another, nor cast one's eye upon lesser state, for Joy embodies All, protector and defender, warding off the caricatures of fate.

Joy abounds aplenty. Here upon the rainbowed heavens, there is no greater delight!

Rapture

United with all Joy, and fused with the Unknown, one's very heart is resurrected from the mortal hold, and transfigured by Love. The soul bows before the luxurious Grace, relinquishing its traumas into the holy embrace.

One ceases to exist, as one is drawn upon the abode of Being. Further and further one is pulled from temporal chain, until one no longer remembers the mortal state. The mind is swept clean, as though one never stepped upon earthly plane, and temporal reality is annihilated beneath the power of the Holy Presence.

Wrung from the fabric of humanly existence, the heart witnesses God's estate. The ego melts into nothingness, as the illusion of mortal separation is revealed, drawing one upon the dwelling place of Union.

Having relinquished the historical image, and traveling along the pathway of the unmarked and unknown, one is prepared to receive the unspeakable and infinite Truth. Guided along the passageways of time and through the gateways of eternity, one joins in the sacred dance, partaking of the mysterious Wonder.

Miraculous Divinity! Unknowable beauty abundant, all radiant, silken light, streaming forth from mystical Heart, and filtering through all life. The Truth stands unshielded, lined in jeweled, crystalline estate. Edifices playfully are erected, building upon the many mansions of delight.

Cascading through eternity, the hearts stand vulnerable and revealed and flow upon creation the balmy winds of exaltation. Rapturous sounds fill the heavens, as angels incantations sing, forming the very fabric of Being.

Holy vision, one becomes the blessed Nothingness, kissed by the silent surrender, and adorned, resting, upon the myriad cushions of divine night. Stars erupt upon the firmament, invoking the deepest passion, all Emotion, without sight. God beckons, and one yearns to depart, alone within eternity's embrace.

Dear God, ecstatic Being, nothing else matters, nothing else takes hold, upon thy Heart, all is Yours, rapturous devotion, the beginning and the end, as all creation sighs, for never alone, one must have You, possessing none other, for none other abides.

Ah, Paradise.

Afterword

This "condition" of mysticism will never be over, for we are of it. We never feel at home elsewhere, but only in the serenity and comfort of our communion with God. We may attempt to make excuses for this state, hoping that it would finally go away and we would then be able to function well in the "real" world. Yet, not only has this never been meant to be, we must no longer yearn for what we are not.

As a human race, we have much to learn. All we can hope

to be is ourselves. Yet, the paradox is that since we all are of God and God, we must know the divine to know the true enactment of the physical. It is this insistent tug from the Infinite which compels us to open our hearts to what God has in store.

All journeys have their markers and their pathways. Even so, and perhaps more so, the ascent to God. Once we tenuously emerge from our shells, we find that many throughout history have shared a similar fate. Spiritual pioneers are guided from above, they must be guided from above for, by definition, they are evolving within a new expression of the same Infinite One. Despite the many varied physical paths, the spiritual path maintains certain shared similarities.

Perhaps our journeys begin with an intense longing, a longing to Know, to find that which transcends the temporal; and a necessity for the comprehension of divine love. It seems that these two conditions occupy our conscious minds for some time. They haunt us, fight with our resistance and fear, and demand a new kind of attention. We are entwined in turmoil, physical despair, and thus a deep inner search.

The passion to Know, and the sincerity of our quest, brings us to a plateau where what we sought was now granted in greater and greater magnitude. That is, at some point the desire and the longing transcends the limited "I" and it was no longer our desire nor our longing—it is The desire and The longing. The intensity of our need to know breaks through the confines of our need to exist, that is, our limited ego selves. This seems to be the first prerequisite for mystical insight. When the yearning for God consumes all else and directs the temporal will to the higher attainment, then we literally exist in another plane of reality. The yearning, however, can only come from the heart and from the love, not from the ego or the will, not from the insecurity of the human condition. It must be pure and untouched, a passionate longing.

It is then that the universe touches us. We are no longer in control. We are anointed from above and all our daily endeavors seem to be part of a greater Plan, a window into the world of God's creative mystery. Every action, every pain, and every joy only further illuminates the sacred splendor of the Blessed Infinite one. This is not to say that we find ourselves hidden on a mountain. Quite the contrary. Our mission is to discern God's pattern in all things, to understand the principles of the Word, and the application of those principles in temporal life.

The suffering is immense and yet it is nothing, being washed within God's heart and soothed upon angel's wings. The test involves the acceptance of suffering and our ability to give and to reach to others in the midst of our own pain and groping. To know the Love we must learn the unconditional ground of commitment, the state of "being there." The suffering is a blessing as it removes the mask of temporal life, revealing the infinite grace and joy.

Mysticism is the magnetism that draws us into Knowing. It is joined with, yet distinct from, great religious insight. Mysticism, however, does not remain in the realm of vision alone, but encompasses the desire to know God as well as attaining mastery of the tools necessary to get There. This is an important and often overlooked point. Mystics are those who not only face the Infinite, but are transformed by it. Each insight beckons the soul's further advancement, challenging those securities which hold dear to human form. As such, one who embarks upon the mystical path, will ultimately learn to function within the paradox of surrender and intense passion, which both direct and channel the immense longing into the concrete physical tests necessary for purification.

Mystical evolution involves the removal of human patterns, the belief in our despair, our historical heritage, and our willful insistence on the paradoxes of human invention. The willingness to love the negative and to see the ultimate illusion of negativity's hold is a key element in spiritual growth. But to transcend the negative, one must be willing to walk through it, to learn its ways, to tackle its insanity and to emerge whole and cleansed.

The process of literally removing negativity and death from the cells of one's body is physically painful. This process seems in one form or another to be part of all mystical journeys, for without the purification of the body and the soul, one cannot maintain rapture with God. Spiritual transformation requires a certainty that transcends faith; this certainly comes after one has already been touched by the Divine Presence and therefore cannot fear. It demands walking in the dark, blindfolded, not knowing where one will land, being willing to shoulder ridicule and deceit; but never giving up, never succumbing to the temptation to return to the ephemeral world of mortal play.

It is this process of coming closer to God that is Life. It is this process that cripples our days and causes us to weep silently and alone. Yet, it is also this process that allows us to heal others, to lift them out of their own darkness, to comfort their souls, and to witness the miracle of transformation. For without self-purging, without the incessant and sometimes brutal call to Truth, one does not progress along the road to the Divine.

What distinguishes ourselves from others in this regard, I do not know. I only know that the passion to know, to love, and to comprehend the Infinite, so that we may ease human suffering, is a constant factor in our lives. This necessity has overwhelmed all other possible endeavors and paled them in comparison. For, without God and infinite knowledge, there is no Life. We are desolate without our Love, and yet this does not mean that we do not still yearn for the human embrace.

Why the human plane is so fraught with paradox, sorrow, and suffering, I cannot answer. But the solution to our condition rests on the ability of all people to confront their own demons, to wrestle with their own dragons, and to slay them with the hand of love. If this can be done, then humanity will understand the mystical journey, where all illusion must be shred from the heart. The illusion is deep and the fear of its power is tangible. Yet, in the moments of mystical insight, one comes to know that ALL negativity is merely transitory and insignificant. One comes to know courage. One gathers the strength to hold the sword of righteousness, born of infinite mercy. And one learns to pray for the destruction of those elements of one's psyche which impede communion with God. One learns to ask for deliverance from the will, from the ego, and from the craving for human survival. One learns to cherish the magnitude and force of the Truth.

God works in mysterious ways. This historical age requires radical methods. We are, I think, to distill the essential from history and from all the great and masterful works so that we will discover that which exists before history. We are to discover the fundamental essence of the Most High in all, the universal foundation. As such, there are those who do not adhere to any tenet, they cannot, for all belief is diminished by the Blessed and Sacred emanation of God. This is so for myself. Rituals and religious rules confine me; social and moral systems appear stagnated and archaic. Infinity moves on. All structures come into being and pass away. Even man's conception of God.

And so, we are compelled to tackle a most profound and exciting issue in our spiritual quest. A new history is being born and we are the architects of its unfolding. We are to shed all the structures of our security, all the trappings of the mind and seek through the virgin state, our original vulnerability, to perceive the Heart of God directly. To do this we must know Love, humility, compassion, commitment, and the unconditional willingness to embrace our destiny. To do this requires an immense shedding of sin and guilt, an acceptance of our grace in God and a willingness to be pioneers upon the seas of unchartered unfolding.

Mystical insight is particularly suited for such a task. For one becomes trained in the abandonment of self-desire and the acceptance of a greater force in life's work. Perhaps spiritual history serves as a precursor for the general condition of humanity. Perhaps the intense communion with God is what we ALL seek and all need, despite physical evidence to the contrary.

These pages were offered as a guide for those who deeply yearn for spiritual meaning in life. It is hoped that by passing on the underlying method of the mystical journey, others will be aided in their own search for the Unknown.

Fashioned from the passion of creation, this book wished to express the melodic aspect of divine Being. It attempted to trace the patterning of God amidst our daily endeavors and to reveal that place within all hearts where our true home resides.

Beginning with a passionate yearning, one evolves along the mystical way, searching among life's ruins for that untouched and holy Truth. For what, beneath all history's trials, can give meaning and stability to life if not this universal Splendor? It is this search for Truth which guides one Home, and where one becomes intoxicated by the Beauty of Love.

The search, which consumes one and becomes everything, draws one closer and closer to divine Heart, and compels one to attempt the arduous path. God is calling, the Infinite beckons the mortal traveler, and there is no choice, but to seek God alone.

It is the love of Truth which provides the necessary strength, allowing the precious, holy, surrender to entrust one's life to the Unknown. Nothing is asked, yet all is given, in the abode of the Heart.

The journey is both simple and exquisitely complex. Passing through the fabrications of the mind and the machinations of history, one arrives at the gateway to the soul. Wandering among the libraries of spiritual knowledge, one remembers and invokes the ancient Memory.

Learning begins in earnest as one turns the pages of Time, skimming over the paragraphs of creation, life after life imprinted in various hue. Much will be seen and the fringes of

Truth glimpsed, as one ascends within the dimensions of the soul.

God's Love abounds and one is drawn upon the abode of Union, into the eternal embrace. No sound disturbs the mighty Presence and all is adorned in the unseen darkness. Flowering open upon Itself, creation enjoins devotion, radiating into form.

Nothing can be spoken of this Truth, only the heart can know its wonders. As such, words can only reflect the Holiness, resonating within the heart's intent.

This is but a small recollection, drawn from the depths of my heart, and fashioned upon the fabric of mortal time. The writing was birthed in total, being neither formed from the intellect nor intended to instruct. These are the experiences within the great Existence of us all, offered with the simple hope that Love shall bind us all to the eternal Heart, and dwelling place of Truth.

It is presented also with the humble hope that those sharing in it be inspired to seek the sacred journey, the enactment of our destiny in God.